Relationships:
Why are they difficult
& what can we do about it?

Avigail Abarbanel

Fully Human Psychotherapy
http://fullyhuman.co.uk

Fully Human Psychotherapy Tools for Life Series
2017-2018

Relationships:
Why are they difficult & what can we do about it?

Fully Human Psychotherapy Tools for Life Series

Other booklets in the series:

- *Grief and Adjustment to Change: A no-nonsense approach*
- *Don't Put Up With Anxiety: Cure it!*
- *Trauma and its Impact: What you need to know.*

First published on Amazon 2018
(Updated: 25th January 2019)

© Avigail Abarbanel — Fully Human Psychotherapy

Author can be contacted via http://fullyhuman.co.uk

Table of Contents

Introduction

There are many relationship texts on the market and they all make a useful contribution. One text I am particularly fond of is the twenty-year-old, *Really Relating: How to build an enduring relationship* by my teachers, Dr David Jansen and Margaret Newman.

David and Margaret were a husband wife psychotherapy team who specialised in relationships. The Jansen Newman Institute (JNI) they founded in Sydney Australia began as a relationship counselling service and developed into a respected and accredited training institute. David and Margaret created 'The School of Marriage', a successful two-weekend programme for couples that ran for many years. It later changed its name to 'Really Relating' to match the title of their book.

I was fortunate to be a student at JNI under David and Margaret in the late nineties. After I graduated and when David and Margaret retired, I was invited to take over the facilitation of the Really Relating programme alongside a male ex-classmate. It was a rewarding and challenging experience that taught me a great deal and that helped increase my confidence as a relationship psychotherapist and a trainer.

In this booklet I do not wish to repeat *Really Relating*. In fact, this booklet is not even specifically about intimate or romantic relationships. It is about *all* adult relationships.[1] My intention is to go right to the heart of relationships and what goes on in them. I aim to discuss topics that are not usually covered in relationship texts. They include the neuroscience that has transformed the field of psychotherapy over the last two decades. This knowledge, or way of thinking, was not available when I was a psychotherapy student. It is a gamechanger in psychotherapy and in understanding relationships.

In one of our Really Relating workshops, a female participant said that she was in a relationship but couldn't convince her partner to attend the workshop with her. She decided to attend on her own to learn what she could. She said it wasn't just about this particular workshop. Her partner absolutely refused to have anything to do with learning about relationships or doing any relationship work at all. She asked us if we had any advice for her.

---

[1] I will cover the topic of parenting, relationships between adults and children, in a separate booklet in this series.

Not knowing the couple or their circumstances it was impossible to give advice. But one thing was clear to us and we did say it to the group. No one can 'fix' an adult relationship on their own. Relationships require *both* partners' participation. Both people have to be *interested*, *committed*, *available* and *able* to participate *equally* in any process intended to enhance the relationship, change things that aren't working or heal what might need healing, with or without professional help.

People who are unable to care enough, reflect, learn, challenge themselves and ultimately change, do not usually make good partners in relationships. For example, if one partner in a relationship raises an issue that is a problem for him or her, it has to become automatically important to the other. "But it's not a problem for me" is not a helpful or caring response. Even if people do not initially understand the other person's issue, even if it's not something that bothers them personally, once it is raised, they have to pay attention. If something is an issue for the person with whom you are in a relationship, it's now an issue for you as well.

When people lack the abilities necessary to participate in healthy and safe relationships it would be virtually impossible to sort anything out with them. Such relationships are usually not safe. It's not only because they can be filled with resentment and hurt, but also because they tend to become stagnant as more and more issues become taboo. The more issues people avoid or tiptoe around, the more likely it is that, over time, trust will erode. In the end it can lead to a 'flattening' of feelings and of the attachment between people. Walking on eggshells around the person with whom you are in a relationship (any relationship) should be a red flag.

I am an idealist. My philosophy in all my psychotherapy work is based on the values of *humanistic psychology*. I believe that we have an innate drive to develop to our full potential and therefore a duty to work towards it and help others do the same. People can survive almost anything. But no one lives a good life if all they do is survive.

According to humanistic psychology the source of most psychological problems is an inability to fulfil our potential. From the perspective of humanistic psychology, psychotherapy isn't just about crisis or 'fixing' people or relationships as if they are broken objects. It's also not about symptom management or 'coping' with a miserable life.

Real psychotherapy is about potential, what is possible for us, individually or in relationships and finding a way to move towards it.

David and Margaret used to say that they weren't promoting one particular model of relationship. They were just responding to what people said they wanted. I'm much less objective. I have an agenda. I believe that good, healthy relationships help us become more of who we are. Good relationships help us develop towards our potential, while bad relationships hold us back. That is in fact how you can tell the difference. If a relationship you are in, whether it is a friendship, a relationship with a sibling or an intimate partner is stopping your development and making you feel stuck, it is not a good sign.

To engage in relationships that provide closeness, safety, space and opportunity for growth and fulfilment, all the people involved have to be reasonably well developed. Immature people who live a shallow life, who avoid and escape as a way of life, or who are just coping and surviving are not available to engage in fulfilling relationships. It's not that they don't want to or that they are 'bad'. They genuinely cannot. For different reasons their brain might not let them.

I am interested in relationships that provide a 'therapeutic' environment for everyone involved. I don't mean that people should be each other's therapists. But I believe that all the relationships we are in need to nurture everyone's growth and development, not just keep them alive. The atmosphere in the relationship is particularly important if there are children involved *and* if people are interested in more than just helping children survive physically.

Relationship therapy is demanding and difficult. There might be three people in the room, but often the room is so full, you can hardly breathe. Each partner in the relationship brings with them the 'ghosts' and presence of many others, they bring their past and present and even their hopes and ideas about the future. This is a lot to manage and it reflects what people are dealing with outside of therapy. Relationships are genuinely complicated. Two people are never just two people and people in relationships are not being silly or bad for having difficulties.

When I work with a relationship the client *is the relationship*. The client is the 'space' between the two people involved. It is created by them and they are both responsible for how well or unwell it is. Relationship therapy is delicate and complex and I love it. It's an amazing experience to see a relationship grow and develop from a space that might have started as unsafe and unhappy to something completely different.

Can everyone do relationships well? I don't think so and it's not a judgment. It's a fact. There are a few neurological capacities that we need in order to be able to engage in good, healthy, resilient and reciprocal relationships. Unfortunately, they don't work well in everyone. I discuss this in some detail in this booklet.

You don't have to be in an intimate relationship to learn about relationships. All human beings participate in many relationships, some more significant than others. All of our relationships, even those that are not so significant, can teach us a great deal about ourselves and what areas we might need to develop and improve in ourselves. We can all develop and do better.

A relatively short booklet can't cover everything there is to say about relationships. I hope what I share here adds to what is already available and that you will find it useful. Some of the topics in this booklet are not covered in other texts and I hope I am offering new perspectives and angles to consider.

I encourage you to read critically, take your time to process and integrate what makes sense to you and what you find useful. Don't just believe me. Refer to your own experience and explore. Whatever your relationship challenges are and whomever the other person happens to be, an intimate partner, a friend, family member, an adult child, a work colleague, it could be helpful to read things together if possible and share information, knowledge and insights.

People are often afraid to bring up topics like love, grief or anger with other adults, especially if this hasn't been a part of the culture in the relationship. If each one of us simply starts talking about things without making a big deal out of it, then it tends not to be such a big deal. We can 'normalise' certain topics that have been perhaps awkward by simply talking about them and inviting others to join us. When was the last time you told a good friend, your brother or sister, a neighbour or a colleague how much they meant to you?

I've heard it so many times, "My brother/father/mother/husband doesn't do feelings. So we never talk about how we feel about each other." All relationships end because we all die at some point. The deepest regrets that people take to their grave tend to be about relationships. Even if it feels awkward, by starting to say certain things to others, we give permission for them to do the same. Some regrets cannot be helped. But I believe we should try to prevent as many regrets as possible while we still can.

I would like all of us to be 'therapeutic' to one another, be safe to be around and help each other grow and be all we can be. I hope this booklet will contribute towards this goal.

~

I welcome feedback on everything I write. You can contact me through my practice website at http://fullyhuman.co.uk. If you are on Facebook you can catch me through my practice Facebook page Fully Human Psychotherapy.

Avigail Abarbanel

November 2018
Scottish Highlands

AN IMPORTANT NOTE

If you believe you are harmed in a relationship right now, your priority should be to protect yourself and any children, other vulnerable people, or even pets who might be affected.

Control and violence, whether physical or emotional, are covered under the definition of 'coercive control', which is now illegal across the UK. Coercive control and bullying can be perpetrated by parents or other relatives, adult children, within religious communities, clubs, organisations, or even in the workplace, not only in close relationships.

If you believe you are the victim of coercive control, if you are bullied, harassed or controlled in any of your relationships, it is vital that you avoid isolation. Make sure that there are people around you to support you, help you to stay safe and contact organisations that can help you.

Harm is caused usually where there is an imbalance of power. Where there is an imbalance of power, therapy is not a priority, safety is.

If you don't have anyone in your life who can support you, there are organisations and services that can. Do not hesitate to contact the police in your area if you are not sure which way to go. The police are well-informed and are able to offer a great deal of support, protection, direction and advice.

What *Is* Relationship?

Relationships are invisible. They cannot be touched, measured, seen, smelled or tasted. Yet they are as real as the book or electronic device you are holding right now. Although they can't be seen like an object, relationships are 'visible' through the impact they have on people. Relationships affect us psychologically, emotionally and physically because they wire and re-wire our brain from the moment we are born and throughout our lives.

A relationship between any two people is much more than two personalities or lives added together. In relationships, **1+1≠2.** In all relationships 'the whole is bigger than the sum of its parts'. Whatever it is that we create with others when we are in relationship, whatever it looks or feels like, it is always much bigger than two lives added together.

If I try to define relationship, capture the essence of what a relationship is, I would say that a relationship is a *process*. A relationship is not a finished 'thing' with a fixed 'shape' or form like a lamp or a chair. A relationship is something that is alive and that keeps changing and adjusting from moment to moment. Even relationships that people describe as stagnant or 'stuck', are still moving and changing, albeit slowly and maybe not in a way that feels good or right.

Despite the fact that relationships do not have a fixed form, they do have boundaries. Like relationships, boundaries are also invisible. People tend to start noticing or thinking about boundaries usually when they are breached or when they don't work so well. If I had to draw a picture to describe a relationship, it would be something like an amoeba. It is there, it exists, it has a membrane, a boundary that holds it together, but it moves and it keeps changing shape.

Relationships are a process where there is a mental exchange between people. When people are in relationship they create a neurological signature inside each other's heads. We wire ourselves into each other's brains, effectively creating a *mental* presence of ourselves inside each other's brains. Everyone with whom we are or were in relationship is quite literally present in our brain. Inside our brain there is a representation of that person and everything that makes up or made up our relationship with them. This is why relationships can continue even when people are apart and do not communicate much and even when people die. In bereavement therapy we often say that the relationship doesn't end when someone dies, it just changes. The person might not be there anymore in the flesh, but they still exist in the brains of those who knew them. As long as we are alive, the circuitry in our brain that is created as a result of our contact with other people remains with us.

Relationships can be more or less involved, they can be more or less intimate, more or less important to us. They can be short-term, like joining-up with someone temporarily to complete a particular project or task, or they can be lifelong, like old friendships, intimate partnerships or family relationships.

Relationships can be happy or unhappy, clear or confusing, close or distant. But whatever they look like, all relationships leave a mark on us through what they wire into our brains. The wiring left inside our brain would play a bigger or smaller role in our life, in a positive or negative way. This depends on how significant the relationship is or was, what it was like and how long it lasted.

We 'move on' quicker from some relationships, while others can take a lifetime to make sense of (rewire and integrate). How long it would take to recover from the end of a relationship depends entirely on what the relationship managed to wire into our brain. It also depends on what we need to do to process it.

Whatever relationships are and whether or not we can define them, we *know* we are relational beings. We don't have a choice about it. We are born into relationships and are raised in relationships. Of all the mammals on this planet, our young are the most vulnerable and take the longest to become independent. We are completely helpless when we are born and depend entirely on others for a very long time. From the moment we are born, whether we like it or not, we have to be in relationship in order to survive.

In addition to survival, we, humans, also have a fundamental need for meaning and purpose. A human life focused entirely on physical survival is miserable and tends to be filled with psychological problems. Relationships with others are therefore crucial, not only for our physical survival but also for the way we continue to develop and the way life will feel and be for us. Relationships can offer a safe, stimulating and inspiring space for us to grow towards our potential, or they can focus only on our physical survival and therefore limit us and compromise our development, thus keeping us unwell.

Our Relational Brain

Our brain is relational. It is 'sculpted' not in isolation and not just by our genetics. To a large extent the human brain is sculpted by relationships. Whatever genetic potential we are born with, how we 'turn out' depends on our environment and in particular, on the kind of relationships available to us.

The most influential relationships, those that leave the most significant and lasting mark on the way our brain is wired, are the ones we are offered earlier in our development. But relationships affect us for better or worse all through life. That's because our brain can change its 'architecture'. It is wired and rewired all though our life and this changes how we think, feel, function, relate, process information, how and what we learn and how we develop. *Everything* about us is affected by this process of wiring and rewiring the brain. This ability of the brain to change its structure and connectivity is called *neuroplasticity*.

If we didn't have neuroplasticity we wouldn't be able to learn anything. Learning is enabled by neurons connecting together, forming new neural pathways and new neural networks. Everything in our brain, all our knowledge, skill, memory, abilities, is contained in neural networks of brain cells that are firing together.

We know our relationships affect how we turn out and the degree to which we can fulfil our potential both from life experience and scientific evidence. The most important evidence that our brains are shaped by relationships comes from neuroscience. But even before neuroscience evolved to what it is today, we knew this from *attachment theory*[2] and studies on attachment, as well as observations in clinical practice and in life in general.

The link between the type of attachment we are exposed to and how we 'turn out' has been validated repeatedly by studies on the brain. Researchers can look into the brains of children who enjoy secure attachment and the brains of children who experience insecure attachment and they can see the differences between them. They can see clear differences in the development, the architecture and

---

[2] Information about attachment and attachment theory is widely available. You also can read about it in my booklet on Anxiety, which is a part of this series. For further exploration on how neuroscience and attachment theory intersect, you can look up writings by Daniel Siegel, Allan Schore or Bruce Perry. There is a growing body of knowledge on this topic.

functioning of the brains of children who have experienced secure or insecure attachment.

What our brain is like on the inside makes us what we are on the outside. The architecture of our brain determines how we feel, behave, what we think and believe, what we are good at and not so good at, how we learn and process information and how we experience ourselves and understand the world around us. The architecture of our brain, in key areas, determines what we call 'mental health'. When we change in some way, for better or worse, it means that something inside our brain has changed. It's not abstract or 'airy fairy'. It's all very physical and very real.

Throughout our life, healthy relationships tend to have a positive impact on us, while relationships that aren't healthy will have a negative impact. *Positive impact* means that healthy relationships wire our brain in a way that leaves us less troubled, worried or afraid. People in healthy relationships tend to feel reasonably secure about themselves and others and the world around them and they tend to be more resilient[3]. This frees up more of their mental resources for development and for reaching their potential.

Negative impact means that unhealthy relationships wire our brain in a way that leaves us more troubled, worried and afraid. People in unhealthy relationships are usually less resilient. Any new setback is likely to chip away even further at their already poor sense of security. As a result, more of their mental resources tend to be diverted to survival and coping, leaving less for the tasks necessary to fulfil their potential.

You can't say that a family, a work environment (or any human environment people spend a lot of time in) are perfectly fine if people in them are not fine. What's on the outside ends up on the inside and this is true for about 80% of people. Anyone who still thinks that how people grow up or how they live shouldn't matter to how they turn out or how they are, is simply out of touch with reality.

We can't help it that things are this way. It's just how we are made. In order for our species to survive, our brain has evolved to create internal wiring that is an 'image' of our external reality. We cannot be

---

[3] Resilience is the ability to recover well and fairly quickly from setbacks. Resilience and psychological wellbeing go hand in hand. The healthier we are psychologically the more resilient we tend to be. When people recover from trauma their resilience improves dramatically. In fact, increase in resilience is one of the 'markers' of recovery from trauma.

oriented well to the outside or interact well with our environment unless our inside matches it. What is wired inside our brain is a physical representation or a neurological 'replica' of the conditions and relationships that are around us[4].

Just leaving a relationship or a place where we suffered, doesn't automatically fix things. That's because significant aspects of the place, the environment, the relationships, what we felt there and anything important about it, are wired into our brain. *Really leaving*, means changing our brain architecture. The phrase "You can take the girl out of the country, but you can't take the country out of the girl" is accurate. To 'take the country out of the girl' or in other words, for the girl to adjust to a new life and not be a product of her previous experience, her neural architecture has to change.

It's incredible to think that relationship, something that's so hard to define, something invisible that exists *between* people, has the ability to shape and change the *physical structure* of the brain. But this is what our brain is like and it is what it means to have a 'relational brain'.

---

[4] The process of wiring our external reality into the brain doesn't just begin when we are born. The new field of epigenetics is now discovering that important aspects of the outside world impact on our very genetics and potential while we are still in our mother's womb. Both mothers and fathers pass on epigenetic information to their baby right at the moment of conception. This means that even our genes are not fixed and can change in response to significant life events.

Although everyone knows, or at least suspects, that our early relationships have a significant and lifelong impact on our development and on our capacity to fulfil our potential, society is still slow to accept this. There are a couple of important reasons for this.

One is the age-old fear of 'blaming the parents'. The highest percentage of child abuse occurs within families. For an untold number of children, the family is where they are harmed and suffer the most. Despite this, the family is still sacred and 'untouchable'. But facts are facts, whether we like them or not. Not all families are safe and not all parents are capable of taking on the complex task of parenting children and nurturing them towards fulfilling their potential. Our earliest relationships sculpt our brain. The wiring we leave home with will determine how we will experience life and what we will be able to achieve in our development. Changing this early wiring later in life is possible but not easy. It is what we do in psychotherapy.

The second reason has to do with neo-liberal, right-wing economic and political cultures which currently predominates much of society and the times we live in. In our time, society keeps promoting the unscientific idea that no matter how people are raised "anyone can succeed if only they work hard and have what it takes"... Many politicians who like to promote this, come from privileged backgrounds. They have often inherited a great deal from their families both in substance and in opportunity and connections. This helps to position them in the right places and advance them regardless of how much talent they really have or whether or not they work hard. They have received a great deal of help to get to where they are. They conveniently ignore this and science and suggest that children who grow up in poverty, neglect, deprivation, low aspirations and trauma and who did not attend expensive private schools and universities, can still do just as well 'if only they try harder'. Holding on to this fictitious, biased view, releases society from doing what is necessary to prevent childhood hardship and help people who, for no fault of their own, were born and raised in difficult circumstances.

Why are relationships difficult?

Relationships are difficult for the same reason that life in general can be difficult for many, if not most people. The truth is, we are not particularly 'well made'.

Something a lot of people are not aware of is that we have three brains, not one. At least two of our brains are not naturally wired particularly well together. It means they don't 'talk' to each other as well as they can. Most readers would be familiar with the experience of how the 'head' and the 'heart' can be in 'conflict', or the experience of 'losing it' when we are triggered, only to wonder a bit later why we did what we did or said what we said. These experiences and others like them are a direct result of having a limbic system that isn't communicating so well with our executive functions.

It is impossible to discuss relationships and what goes wrong with them without discussing these two brains, what they are, how they work and how they interact with one another.

The 'Triune (three) Brain Model' was developed by the neuroscientist Paul MacLean in the 1960s.

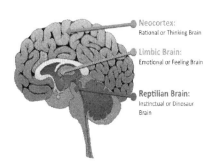

Our three brains more or less represent the stages of evolution of life on this planet: from reptile to mammal and then to human, a uniquely complex and self-aware mammal.

Each of our brains has evolved to handle increasingly complex tasks. MacLean believed that our three brains have different 'mentalities' and that they are not linked together or 'talk to each other' as well as they can. He was right and a great place to observe this is in the way we function in relationships.

The Reptilian Brain

If your reptilian brain (also called the 'cerebellum' or brain stem) is working then you are alive and breathing. The reptilian brain is the 'control centre' for all of our automatic (autonomic) physical functions. These are the functions that tick along in the background and keep the body going. Our immune system, digestion, heart and lung functions for example, are all regulated in the reptilian brain.

Damage to the brain stem can be disastrous because it can cause some or all of the autonomic functions to stop. This can result in people going into a 'vegetative' state.

In therapy we don't worry so much about the reptilian brain. If the client is alive and breathing, we know the reptilian brain is working as it should. It's our other two other brains that are much more significant for therapy and for how we participate in relationships.

The Limbic (Mammal) Brain

The limbic brain or system is our mammal brain. It sits on top of the reptilian brain and is located in the middle of our skull divided between the two hemispheres.

The limbic brain is the brain we have in common with all the other mammals on this planet. It is a very old brain, about two hundred million years old. It is more or less complex in different types of mammals. In humans it is especially complex.

If the limbic brain had an 'agenda', 'mission' or 'purpose' it would be *the survival of our species*. It's not 'interested' if we are happy or not, if we are good or bad, or if our life is particularly fulfilling, happy or satisfying. Our limbic brain works in the service of nature. It 'cares' only that we survive long enough to procreate, protect our young so they live long enough to have more babies, so that our species continues to exist.

The limbic system (working together with the reptilian brain) is responsible for triggering and regulating our 'fight'-'flight'-'freeze' responses. These are the ancient and hard-wired instinctual reactions to threat and danger that have helped our species survive so well on a hostile planet. When we face a threat, the amygdala in the limbic brain raises the alarm. This triggers a cocktail of chemicals (adrenaline and cortisol) to flow into our blood so that different muscle groups and functions can activate to facilitate the responses of fighting, fleeing or freezing. It's all intended to ensure that we survive an immediate threat and go on to live another day.

Our survival instincts

Fight

If we are supposed to fight off a threat, our upper body will become tense and our muscles will get ready for action. We will feel a lot of energy in our upper body as our arms get ready to push something or someone off, or to fight.

When the 'fight' response is triggered, people can demonstrate several times their normal strength. When people get angry and feel the blood rush up to their heads and their upper body it's because it's exactly what it does.

Anger is the emotion associated with the 'fight' response. It is part of the mechanism that activates our fight instinct and that mobilises our body to push away or fight off a threat.

Flight

If the response our limbic brain chooses is to flee, the bottom half of the body will become activated, the muscles in the legs will tense up, ready to run. Our digestive system which takes enormous amount of energy will shut down temporarily and so will our immune system. Our bowels and bladder will try to empty because running with empty bowels and bladder makes us lighter on our feet and we can run faster. More of our ancestors were able to flee successfully when their bowels were empty. That's why this ability or instinct is still with us.

When people are afraid they can feel the blood drain out of their faces, have a 'sinking' feeling in their guts or feel their legs shaking. This is because it's exactly what happens to them physically as the different systems in their body adjust quickly to the need to flee from danger.

Fear is the emotion associated with the flight (fleeing) response. It helps activate the instinct to flee and mobilise the right parts of the body to help us get as far away from a threat, as quickly as possible.

Freeze

Freezing (also called 'dorsal', or horizontal 'dive') probably has a lot to do with playing dead. The body goes into a mild shock-like state and wants to collapse to a horizontal state. Our bodily functions slow down and our skin would feel cold to the touch.

Some of our ancestors survived by appearing dead to potential predators who didn't eat dead things and preferred to kill their prey and consume it fresh. Enough of our ancestors survived thanks to this ability, which is why it is also still with us. I have often wondered if the emotional experience that is associated with the 'freeze' response is a kind of **numbness**.

＆

As we fight, run away or freeze, we use up the adrenaline in our system. If we are successful and survive the threat, the body and the brain go back to a calm, resting state. When we are not under threat we can relax and do what sophisticated mammals do when they are relaxed, play and have fun, relate, have sex, groom, tend to daily tasks like finding food, eat, look after their homes, explore, create, learn or invent something new.

The biggest enemy of the limbic system is death. Each individual in our species has evolved to have a profound fear of dying. This has kept our ancestors alive long enough to make sure our species is still here. If each individual in a species is sufficiently afraid of death it increases the survival chances of the whole species. Imagine a species where 80% of the individuals don't care much if they live or die. Such a species is less likely to survive on a planet filled with dangers.

Individuals do not matter to nature except in their contribution to keeping their species alive. Individuality, uniqueness, or how individuals feel or experience their life, do not matter in terms of species survival.

The limbic brain also enables mammals to bond with other members of their own species and members of other species and form *attachment*. Some mammals are able to cooperate and work as groups. Depending on the species there are degrees of cooperation and there are rules and social structures that regulate how mammal groups function together. All of this is in the service of the survival of the species.

The limbic brain is a clever and complex brain, capable of learning fast, especially when threat and fear are involved. The limbic brain is fear-based because we have evolved on a harsh and dangerous planet and being fearful and cautious helped us survive better. If you are afraid, you are more likely to be careful and watchful and not take unnecessary risks. Our limbic brain is primed and *fine-tuned to fear*. Everything that's ever happened to us, everything we have experienced, is wired into our limbic system, especially if it was significant to our survival and was associated with fear or threat.

Our strongest attachment to other people, things or places is directly related to our survival. Safety is the key to survival, so we develop the strongest attachment where we instinctively perceive that we are safest.

Life was hard for early humans and it's easy to see this even from observing ourselves right now. Our ancestors were running around in rabbit skins in the cold or the heat, in rain, hail or snow, often in inhospitable environments with many dangers from the natural world and from other groups. They had to compete over food and shelter with other species and with other intelligent and possibly dangerous primates who existed alongside our species.

With little control over their environment our ancestors had to make the most of it to survive. Food wasn't always available and getting it was hard and often dangerous work. Human lived alongside large predators and there is evidence now that we were a significant source of food for some large predatory species. Survival wasn't guaranteed. The environment was unpredictable and long-term stability in any area of life was rare.

Different types of mammals benefit from cooperation up to a point. Shortage of food and the presence of constant danger do not necessarily bring out the best in individual mammals. They would easily kill, abandon each other to die of hunger or be captured by a predator just to save themselves.

They are not 'evil'. Evil is a human idea. They don't do it 'deliberately'. This is just a result of the struggle to survive in an uncertain and dangerous environment.

Those who survive longer get to pass on their genes to the next generation. Those who die before they had a chance to procreate, don't. In a dangerous and difficult environment, the stronger, more aggressive or cunning individuals probably survived longer. It is their genes, including the genes responsible for cunning, ruthlessness or aggression that would then be passed on generationally. This works while it works... When it stops working, when abilities a species has no longer help it to survive because the environment has changed in a significant way, the species will either be reduced dramatically in numbers or become extinct. If there is enough time, it might evolve to adapt to new conditions in order to continue to survive.

Feelings / Emotions

To the limbic brain, safety is associated with survival and the absence of safety could mean death. The limbic brain's job is to determine whether we are safe or not. It works together with the reptilian brain and uses our five senses to check continuously what's going on inside of us and around us. The limbic system 'reports back' what it finds through our *emotions* or *feelings* (I use both words to mean the same thing).

There is nothing mysterious or 'airy fairy' about emotions. Emotions are information. They are the limbic brain's ancient language, the way it tries to communicate what is going on in order to increase our chances of survival[5].

There is no such things as 'good' or 'bad', 'right' or 'wrong' feelings. All emotions are *information* and they are all equally valid. The limbic brain in most people works exactly as it is meant to and does exactly what it has evolved to do. An uncomfortable emotion means that our limbic brain has a good reason to believe we are in danger. An uncomfortable feeling, any uncomfortable feeling, is an alert, a signal from our limbic brain that we might be facing a potential threat to our survival.

Regardless of whether there is a real threat in the present (facing a predator, violence, bullying, control or other abuse) or whether it is an old threat wired into our limbic brain from our past, *all our emotions have to be taken seriously*.

Because we are a self-aware mammal we *know* we are feeling something when we feel it. We also tend to worry about what we feel, especially if it is unpleasant. Other animals just feel what they feel and act on their feeling instinctively. When they're happy they're happy, when they're sad, they're sad. They don't try to understand their feelings and they don't worry about them.

Emotions are not our enemy, but it is emotions that keep me in my job and that people always complain about when they come to therapy.

---

[5] I cover emotions in detail in my booklet on anxiety: *Don't Put Up With Anxiety: Cure it!*

It is almost always emotions that people blame for their problems individually and in relationships. The only reason emotions are a problem for most people is simply because we are taught the wrong lesson about them. I don't blame parents because parents cannot teach what they don't know. But most of us grow up without knowing what emotions are and how to handle them correctly. We do have the knowledge now and it's never too late to learn. It's especially important in relationships and for people who interact with children and young people.

Poor emotional skill is one of the main causes of relationship problems. One of the most common mistakes people make is to try to 'fix' or change other people's feelings. People tell me all the time how much they wish others would just listen to them instead of try to 'solve their problem', offer advice, try to distract or 'make them feel better'. Most of the time there are good intentions behind this but it is unhelpful.

We all need our feelings and inner experience to be *validated* not changed. Validating people's feelings calms down the limbic brain. This enables people to engage their higher (executive) functions and find their own solutions. When we are validated by others and when we validate ourselves, it sends a message to the limbic brain that it has been heard and that the information the emotions contain has been received.

> Validation means telling someone else that what they are feeling is OK.

Generalising, Predicting & Projecting Forward

Danger and its internal representation, fear, are incredibly effective and fast teachers. Like all mammals, we have developed certain skills to increase our chances of survival. For example, we learned to generalise and try to *predict* and *project forward* from significant experiences in order to survive better, especially but not exclusively around danger.

Generalising is assuming that one event or one example of something tells us how things are in general.

Predicting makes us believe we know what's going to happen next because it's happened before. This is particularly effective when what happened was bad or frightening. We are the descendants of those who managed to survive the challenges of their environment partly because they were good at predicting trouble.

I get annoyed when I hear that some therapists tell their clients that they 'catastrophise', that is they expect the worst. This shows a lack of understanding of our limbic functions. Of course, we catastrophise! That's what he limbic brain has evolved to do. Expecting the worst-case scenario has helped our species survive on a dangerous planet. What else do people expect from those who have experienced a lot of misfortune, hardship or trauma in their life? They would have to have an impaired brain to do otherwise. 'Catastrophising' means the limbic brain is doing its job.

Projecting forward is assuming that what is now, will continue to be. For example, if we feel a certain way now, we expect to feel this way always. Projecting forward is a mechanism that gives us the illusion of control over our environment and circumstances and therefore a sense of safety.

If I think that what is now always will be, then I feel more comfortable that I know what's going on and what I need to do. The limbic brain does not feel secure when things are unpredictable and when it does not feel in control of its circumstances. It has evolved to do everything it can to minimise unpredictability. It expects things to continue on the same path they have always been and if they don't, it triggers a sense of danger and enormous insecurity.

One example that readers might be familiar with is when people are depressed, anxious or grieving and they worry that they will always feel this way. They often say they cannot imagine ever feeling any different. This is caused by our projecting forward mechanism. When I reassure a client that things will get better for them and they won't always feel the way they do now, it can be confusing. I know I am speaking to their limbic brain and that it is simply projecting forward from what is now.

The client's limbic brain will only listen to me up to a point and only believe me if I have some credibility. This plays out in relationships when things are difficult. It's not simple for our limbic brain to believe that things will be better or different when millions of years of limbic evolution tell us we can expect what is now to continue the same way.

Generalising, Predicting & Projecting Forward in Relationships

"My mind is made up. Don't confuse me with facts."
— Anonymous

The otherwise natural survival skills of generalising, predicting and projecting forward can be problematic in relationships. Having been hurt in a relationship can cause people to try to avoid relationships or be suspicious of new people. Even if there is no evidence that a new person or relationship are likely to be hurtful, what is wired inside our brain would tell us otherwise.

People who grew up with insecure attachment in a painful or dangerous home environment would naturally expect to feel exactly the same whenever they bond with someone new or find themselves in a new group, social or professional. It's not something they *choose* to do, it's what is naturally wired into their mammal brain.

Remember that we do not interact with the world directly. We interact with the world through existing circuitry in our brain that represents our reality. Every new experience is compared with whatever is already wired in our brain's pre-existing 'database'. When we experience something new, our brain automatically begins to look for the right 'box' to fit the new experience into. In other words, all new experiences are compared with something that is already pre-wired and are classified accordingly. This helps us make sense of things quickly. If we can quickly classify a furry animal with big teeth as a dangerous predator, instead of taking time to assess what it is every time we come across it, this gives us an immediate advantage. This ability is still with us because it has helped our ancestors survive better.

If we encounter something new that does not exist in our pre-wired database, we are conditioned to be suspicious and feel insecure and uncomfortable about it. We have no infrastructure for the new experience and therefore have no idea how to react to it. The default position is to view something new as potentially risky or threatening until we have evidence to the contrary. All new experiences, even if they are objectively positive and even if we ourselves initiated them, require time to adjust the old circuitry, or to create new circuitry. It's not an option. It's how the brain works.

If in her childhood a woman experienced putdowns, criticism, violence and abuse, this is what will be wired into her brain. This will mean that being in a group, in a family or even just living in a house with other people, can feel dangerous. This is so even if the dangerous people or the abuse are no longer present. We carry our pre-wired reality with us wherever we go.

At some point in life this woman might meet a nice partner who is loving, kind and values her. Instead of feeling immediately happy (why wouldn't she when everything is really quite perfect?) she is more likely to feel suspicious and uncomfortable. This woman is not stupid but her mammal brain does not contain any wiring for a relationship where she is safe, valued, loved and respected.

As dangerous as abusive relationships are, they are much more familiar to her because they are wired into her brain. She recognises them, knows how to be in them and how to survive them. Everything in this woman's brain is wired to recognise an abusive relationship but not a safe or loving one. She doesn't know what the good relationship is or how to be in it. It makes no sense to her. To the ancient limbic brain familiar means safe (even if it isn't) and unfamiliar means unsafe (even if it is)...

Most people aspire for something better than what they had before. But when we move from bad experiences to good ones (or just from previous experiences to new ones) we must allow ourselves time to adjust before we can relax into our new and better reality and enjoy it. The time it takes either to adjust old circuitry or create new circuitry to contain the new experience feels intensely insecure and uncomfortable. All adjustment of brain circuitry following a big change feels this way[6].

Imagine how hard it is for young children whose life experience is so limited. From the moment we are born our brain frantically begins to build our 'inner database' of experiences. Children's brains wire themselves phenomenally fast so that they can be well oriented to their environment and survive it. This is the reason why our experience appears 'normal' to us. Not to wire our reality fast enough means being out of step with it and therefore potentially in danger. Everything that is 'out there' will end up being wired inside our brain and not having enough life experience means that the limbic brain feels insecure.

---

[6] This topic is covered in detail in my booklet on grief and adjustment to change.

Generalising, predicting & projecting forward can make us poor judges of our reality. Changing and adjusting our internal circuitry is possible and we do it all the time. Depending on the magnitude of the adjustment, it can be a complex and intensely uncomfortable process[7].

Rather than wait and collect evidence about what is really going on (which can take time during which we feel insecure and uncomfortable) and then create a theory about it, we often do the opposite. We impose our existing 'theory', the existing inner image of the reality that is pre-wired into our brain, on the new reality and ignore the evidence that proves that it is not in fact the same at all[8].

The phrase, "Don't confuse me with facts, I know what I believe" describes this perfectly. To be able to adjust to new situations and rewire our brain, we need tolerance for the intense discomfort and insecurity that new experiences and the need to adjust our circuitry can bring with them.

We have the ability to resist adjustment by deciding we don't want to do it. Our *intention* plays a huge part in the way our brain responds. We are likely do much better at learning another language if we have the *intention* of learning it. Just having an intention isn't enough, but it is a necessary first step to engaging with any process that requires wiring and rewiring of brain circuitry.

We can resist engaging with new information that challenges what we already believe (what's already wired). We can ignore it or dismiss it as unimportant so that we don't have to pay attention to it. By doing this, we can spare ourselves the intense discomfort that comes with changing our brain circuitry.

I might think I know what someone 'is like' when in fact I know very little about her or him. I might pick up on one thing the other person said or did, or they might look like someone I used to know and 'bingo', 'he is just like so and so...' But is he really? Have I given myself a chance to meet this new person with fresh eyes and an open brain, or am I pre-

---

[7] It is why 'real' psychotherapy is such a challenging and demanding process. In real psychotherapy we work to change the architecture of the brain. Without changing our brain architecture no real change can happen in us.

[8] This is precisely why science and the scientific method were invented. Our limbic brain makes us pretty lousy scientists because we often try to fit the outside to what's already inside. Science and the scientific method prevent people from doing this. If scientists have a theory but it's not backed up by evidence, they change it or replace it with a theory that fits reality better. Good scientists do not get rid of the evidence in order to hold on to what they 'believe'.

judging because it's what is wired inside my limbic brain and it feels easier and safer to make assumptions?...

It can be a huge problem in relationships when people think they know each other and what to expect from one another when in fact they are prejudging because of existing wiring.

Parents who project a pre-existing image of someone else onto a child, can do harm. They force the child into a pre-existing template and don't allow the child to develop into the person he or she can naturally become. People feel it when they are seen as someone they are not. It is not only confusing, it can also be quite harmful.

People often act on their assumptions in the same way they acted when the original experience was first wired. For example, people can withdraw, become hostile, defensive or seductive in a way that is disproportionate or inappropriate. These behaviours can be a product of the past rather than the present and they are likely to cause harm and conflict.

The Neo Cortex & the Prefrontal Cortex (PFC)

Our third brain is called the Neo Cortex, 'neo' from the Greek for 'new'. The neo-cortex is the newest and largest brain we have. It sits on top of and covers the two older brains. The neo cortex allows us to perform functions that are uniquely human. It has made it possible for us to invent technology, perform complex tasks, develop language and writing and create the complex reality we live in now with everything that it contains.

The part of our neo cortex that is most significant to how we are in relationships is our *prefrontal cortex* (PFC), aka 'the executive brain'. It is located at the front part of the neo cortex. If you draw a vertical line from the middle of your eyebrows upwards, it's more or less right there in the middle on both sides. In addition to the limbic brain, the PFC is the most important part of the brain for therapy and for what we call growth, recovery and wellbeing in general.

The prefrontal cortex is the central processing unit of the entire brain. It processes and organises an amazing amount of information that comes from all over the brain and it coordinates our most advanced functions. It's our PFC and the executive functions it gives us that make our species unique and makes us 'human' (as opposed to being 'just' a mammal). It is the part of us that gives us the sense of being 'adult'.

The PFC is something of a mystery. It is the latest part of the brain to develop in our species and also in each one of us. It begins to develop as soon as we are born but fully 'kicks in' if you like (and if all goes well) around the age of fifteen[9].

Observant adults would recognise the moment their child suddenly becomes more conscious of others and more aware of themselves. It's as if suddenly someone presses the switch and turns on the light. It can happen in an instant. One minute they are still a child and the next minute they are different. Children experience this as a moment when everything changes for them. It can be incredibly frightening to become self-aware and suddenly see the things that are 'wrong' around you and become aware that you are suffering. Many young people who are not brought up the right way, often begin to exhibit psychological and behavioural problems and 'act out' after their prefrontal cortex has kicked in. They suffered before but they just felt it and reacted. Now they *know* what they are feeling and it can be overwhelming without the right support.

The prefrontal cortex is highly specialised. It can easily be damaged or compromised by drugs or alcohol. Its functions, as far as we know cannot be replaced or taken over by any other part of the brain. Once the PFC is gone it's really gone. The prefrontal cortex is so important in human relationships and in psychotherapy, that looking after it should be everyone's priority.

The prefrontal cortex gives us a long list of incredible, uniquely human abilities. All of these abilities are crucial for our functioning as mature individuals and in relationship with others. They are called 'executive' or 'higher' functions.

Compassion — We seem to be naturally compassionate when we operate from the prefrontal cortex. I'm not sure why that is, but it is what I have observed in my work with every single client. It's easy and natural to experience compassion towards everyone and everything when you have really accessed your PFC.

---

[9] I have heard a few stories over the years of incredible young children who seem to have executive abilities like empathy and insight that appear far beyond their years. I suspect that in a small number of children the prefrontal cortex 'turns on' earlier than fifteen.

Unconditional love — The prefrontal cortex gives us the capacity to love others in a mature way and without judgment or need. The kind of love we experience from our PFC does not depend on what others give or do for us, whether or not they help us survive, who they are or even if they love us back. We just seem to be able to love everything and everyone unconditionally.

Attunement and empathy — The prefrontal cortex enables us to be attuned to what someone else is going through. It's a kind of *aware sensitivity* to other people's inner experience. Dan Siegel[10] talks about the ability to make others 'feel felt'. The PFC is the part of the brain that enables us to communicate to others that we *see* them and their inner experience and that we are *with* them. We can often do this with just a look.

If you are on the receiving end of someone else's attunement, you just know. You *feel* that the other person *sees* you. Empathy from the prefrontal cortex is somewhat different to the limbic brain's ability to *resonate* with other people's inner states, or feel their feelings (see section on the Mirror Neurons). You can feel someone else's feelings and not care much, or you can even get annoyed or frightened by them, reject the other person or shut yourself off from them.

The PFC gives us the ability to *care* about what someone else is feeling and the instinctive knowledge of how best to be with them in that moment to maintain not only their physical wellbeing but their wholeness.

Self-awareness — Self-awareness is the ability to look inward and 'see' what we are feeling or doing. Without self-awareness it is difficult if not impossible to change or grow. Self-awareness can make us suffer more. When we become aware that we are not living well, that things are not right around us or in the world, that we are not happy or fulfilled, that we are betraying our own values or principles, or that we are doing harm, it will make us feel guilty and uncomfortable. Being self-aware comes with a responsibility to ourselves and to others, but it's a responsibility that our PFC can handle.

---

[10] See Daniel Siegel's book, *Mindsight*.

Planning and decision making — The prefrontal cortex gives us the ability to take on board a lot of information, analyse it and make *long-term* plans and adult rational decisions. In this we consider not only what affects us directly or immediately. We consider the 'bigger picture', other people and circumstances as well as the long-term consequences. Unlike the limbic brain, the PFC is not limited to past experience and a pre-wired 'database'. It seems to have a built-in ability and flexibility to consider many options and be creative about possibilities or solutions to problems that we might never have seen or experienced before.

Intuition — Intuition is something that most people experience from time to time. It is the ability to take in information we don't even know we're taking in, process and analyse it extremely fast and come up with a solution, an answer or an idea. Intuition works so fast, that we don't recall collecting the information, sorting through it or analysing it. We don't know how we know that this was the right thing to do. It feels like a 'knowing' that comes out of nowhere.

The older I get the more I trust my intuition. The limbic brain doesn't trust what it can't see, sense, remember, track and grasp. To trust our intuition means that we need to be able to let our PFC be in charge. To our limbic brain, an intuition that turned out to be correct can feel like 'magic', a miracle, something that is unlikely or impossible.

Perspective and objectivity — The prefrontal cortex gives us the ability to 'stand back' from a situation or from ourselves and look at it from a broader and more objective perspective than our limbic brain is able to do. Because the limbic brain is so focused on our individual survival every moment, it can be 'selfish', 'self-absorbed' and 'self-focused'. Our limbic brain would tend to judge every situation according to how it affects *us* or how well it serves *our particular interests (survival)*. Our PFC however, can look at how we each fit in the 'bigger picture' and make us know that we are not the most important or only person around.

Emotional and behavioural regulation — The PFC is built to interact with our emotions and regulate them. Emotions are information and the prefrontal cortex needs this information in order to make good decisions. It has the capacity to listen to them and understand what they are trying to say, then reassure the limbic brain that the information has been successfully communicated and received. This enables the limbic brain to calm down, knowing that things will be taken care of.

The PFC is able to regulate our behaviour. It can choose actions and solutions that aren't just habitual 'kneejerk reactions' pre-wired by our past experience and our species' evolution. Even if you feel intense anger, when your PFC is properly engaged, you will not 'lash out' at someone else. You'll be able to feel your anger but you will have positive ways of attending to it and expressing it in a non-harmful way.

If your anger gives you useful information about something that is happening now, you will be able to address that situation with clarity, wisdom, consideration for the welfare of others and perspective. If your anger provides information about the past, you will take the appropriate and proportionate action to help yourself integrate that past so it's no longer triggered as much. The limbic brain is reactive, without the PFC to regulate it, the limbic brain would tend to react and act out what it feels.

Fearlessness — I have noticed that when people operate out of their PFC they seem not to be motivated by fear. The PFC does not seem to have the same fear-based herd instinct that our mammal brain has and it doesn't seem to 'feel' fear. In fact, it doesn't *feel* much at all except a kind of benevolent concern and compassion for everyone and everything, irrespective of whether they are members of our particular group or tribe.

If you look closely when people say they only have one or two options in a situation, you'll almost always find that they're afraid. Those limited choices usually come from the ways we have adapted to deal with threat or fear in our childhood. Some people might withdraw when they are scared, others might lash out, eat, smoke or drink. They might try to please or placate the person that triggers them, or otherwise comply and choose the path of least resistance.

The limbic system would tend to choose the option with the least amount of discomfort because it is perceived as the least risky to our physical survival. If people 'gang up' on someone at work, would we join the gang, or would we risk rejection from the rest of the group and stick by that person? Our limbic brain would tell us to put ourselves first, but our PFC would tell us to do the right thing and would not feel afraid to do it. Our PFC would guide us to act in ways that are not motivated by fear.

Need for meaning and purpose — This a particularly interesting and tricky function of our PFC. As mammals we don't need a reason or justification to be alive. We are born, so here we are. We naturally wish to live as long as possible, possibly for ever. We have no individual purpose except to make sure we live long enough to pass on our genes, so that our species continues.

Our PFC seems to have other ideas, or another 'agenda'. It demands that we have a purpose, a reason for our existence. It gives us a sense of mission. It tells us that we have to do something with our life, not just exist. It seems that, according to our PFC, the survival of our species is not enough of a reason for humans to exist. Existence has to mean something.

It can be a problem for mammals that 'merely existed' for hundreds of millions of years, to suddenly 'wake up' to feeling that survival isn't enough and that life also has to mean something. Our PFC won't allow us to live as unaware mammals who just exist, without paying a heavy price. It is an extraordinary and difficult contradiction to carry inside one head.

People who have a well-developed PFC (probably most people), have a natural sense of 'mission' about their lives and a sense of direction and purpose.[11] They might have a feeling that they have some kind of a duty to use their lives for a purpose. As mammals, our purpose is given to us by nature. Our PFC gives us the option of *choosing* what our purpose is or should be. Whatever we choose and however we decide to use our life, our skills and our talents, it also has to be *meaningful* and it has to be consistent with our values. If it isn't, we feel a conflict within ourselves.

If you have been in a well-earning job but begin to feel like you are not making any difference, that you don't care much about what you are doing and that you should be doing something that is more

---

[11] To what degree we would be able to fulfil our mission, follow our sense of direction and fulfil our potential, will depend on how integrated our limbic brain is with the functions of our PFC. (See next chapter Neural Integration.)

meaningful, something that 'matters' more, that's your prefrontal cortex 'talking' to you.

If you have always worked hard and put your work ahead of your family, then one day *realise* that you are doing it, it's your PFC talking to you. It's telling you that you have an important purpose to relate to your children properly, spend time with them and not neglect them.

Purpose and meaning are unique to each individual, but it almost always seems to benefit others. It makes us feel that we are living the 'right' life. The PFC is not satisfied with just living for ourselves or just existing. Our life has to be used for the benefit of others.

Higher-level spirituality — The prefrontal cortex gives us the ability to have a spiritual life without being religious and without having a particular deity to worship or a ritual to perform. We don't need someone in authority to tell us what is right or wrong, how to think about ourselves, life or the universe, what to believe or what to do. We just know for ourselves.

Unlike the fear-based limbic system, the prefrontal cortex is fearless and has no need for certainty. It is quite OK with the unknown and can embrace it.

Whether or not there is something out there in the universe (I personally believe there is) it seems to me that the 'antenna' dealing with this is in the prefrontal cortex. It's the PFC that gives us the ability to perceive something bigger than ourselves and feel a connection to it.

Our limbic brain is Earth focused and fear-based. Any religion it can inspire tends to be fear-based and survival-focused. The prefrontal cortex can reach beyond our evolutionary experience. Albert Einstein described the difference between our limbic and prefrontal abilities when he said:

"A human being is a part of the whole called by us universe, a part limited in time and space. He experiences himself, his thoughts and feelings as something separated from the rest, a kind of optical delusion of his consciousness. This delusion is a kind of prison for us, restricting us to our personal desires and to affection for a few persons nearest to us. Our task must be to free ourselves from this prison by widening our circle of compassion to embrace all living creatures and the whole of nature in its beauty."

Conscience, personal ethics and morality   Our prefrontal cortex gives us what we call a conscience. It lets us *know* when we do something wrong and makes us *care* about it. We don't need parents, the police, the law or anyone else to tell us when we do wrong. We know and we care for the 'right' reasons.

If we all operated from the prefrontal cortex most of the time, we wouldn't need a criminal justice system to tell us that it's not OK to break into someone else's home and take their things. We would just know. If our politicians, civil servants or corporate leaders were able to operate from their PFC much more of the time, they would be able to take responsibility for their mistakes rather than deflect, avoid and look for scapegoats. They would also be motivated by more than just self-interest to improve themselves and make amends when they committed a crime, acted immorally or carelessly.

It's our limbic brain that needs a criminal justice system, laws and law enforcement. If we all acted out of our PFC most or all of the time, we probably wouldn't need laws to help us live in groups in a way that is careful, safe and respectful of everyone.

The PFC makes us feel guilt and regret, gives us the ability to own up, take responsibility and make amends, sometimes at a great cost to us. But it's OK because it is the right thing to do out of concern for others. When you witness real courage, someone standing up for others or for what is right, what you are seeing is the PFC in action.

The limbic brain might know that we did something wrong, but like everything else limbic, this too is motivated by fear rather than the ability to grasp our impact on others. Children are predominantly limbic. They know when they're doing something wrong. They can feel guilty when they know that they broke the rules. Children will see that a parent is upset because of something they did. But they will tend to worry about how things affect *them*. "Will mum stop loving me if she is upset with me?" or "Mum and dad might not take care of me if they are unhappy with me".

The limbic brain can make us resent anyone who *makes us* feel guilty. From a limbic point of view, we would rather do something wrong but not be told about it and not be confronted with the impact it had. If people operate from their limbic brain they can lash out at the very people they hurt because guilt makes them feel uncomfortable and they don't want to feel like this.

Awareness of how we affect others — Our prefrontal cortex makes us aware that we are not more important than others. It gives us the ability to be recognise and care about the impact that our behaviour has on other people. It looks like the PFC makes it possible for us to put the welfare of others ahead of our fears. It makes us able to take in feedback about our behaviour and change it so that we are more careful and less harmful.

We are not just focused on how things affect us directly and don't look at every situation from the limbic viewpoint of whether it's good or bad for *us*.

Presence —Presence is the ability to be fully 'present' for someone else without being motivated by our own needs. It's the ability to make our awareness *available* for someone else as a conscious choice. Most psychotherapists know that presence is crucial for therapy to be effective and they do their best to offer this to clients. We know that being present for someone else has an incredibly healing effect. How well any of us can do this depends on our ability to operate reliably from our PFC.

Presence makes us *safer* for others because we are not *caught up* in our own limbic world, our 'agenda', our needs and fears, our pre-wired past, our thoughts and our feelings. Presence is unconditional. It allows others to feel *seen* and *noticed* fully and accurately.

For me, this is linked with attunement. Our PFC allows us to be properly attuned to someone else, notice how they are as a whole being and let them know that we see them. (I am curious to know what we would see if we scanned the brains of two people sitting together when one or both are truly present for the other.)

Identity and sense of self — This is our sense of uniqueness, of our individuality and our sense of having a unique contribution that only we can make because of what makes us what we are. It's the ability in us to know that we are who we are.

The limbic brain's sense of identity can be a little fuzzy and unclear. It will shift and change depending on the situation we are in and how safe or unsafe we feel. Children do not have a strong sense of self. They do their best to adapt to their environment to maximise their chances of survival. In the limbic brain we have a drive to be accepted by our group, or else we risk being tossed out of the cave to die of hunger in the cold. If what the group demands is to be quiet and agree with the leader, that's what the limbic brain will do. The antelope that looks and behaves like all the other antelopes and stands in the middle of the herd is less likely to be caught up by a lion than the one that is too curious and goes exploring by itself.

The sense of identity we have from in the PFC seems to be consistent across situations as if it is more 'solid'. It makes sense because the PFC is not fear-based. We are always ourselves and can behave consistently across situations according to our values and principles no matter who we are with or what the situation is and even when we are under threat.

Clarity — Our thinking from the prefrontal cortex seems to be clear and crisp. We just *know* what we know and feel quietly calm about it. Our thoughts are clear and we are also able to communicate them clearly and quietly to others without emotional intensity and without a need to convince anyone of anything. We don't feel an urgent need to make others think or believe the same as we do.

The capacity for imagination beyond our experience — The limbic brain's imagination is limited by its pre-wired experience. That's probably why when we make decisions from our limbic brain, we often recreate what we know. As I explained earlier, someone who grew up in a violent family might end up in a violent relationship as an adult. It's not because they are stupid or don't understand that they are suffering. But the limbic brain does not know what is possible other than what is already wired into it.

A well-developed prefrontal cortex will give us the ability to imagine 'the impossible', the 'unimaginable', see possibilities that seem beyond reach, see things that we have never experienced. It will also give us the drive and creativity to realise a seemingly impossible vision. If, as a species, we want to experience world peace, if we want kindness, abundance and compassion as the guiding principles for our societies, we have to rely on prefrontal cortex imagination.

At the moment, as a species, we are making largely limbic decisions. We cannot see beyond our experience and can't imagine a world without war, without vicious competition over resources, without danger, suffering, without a split between the 'haves' and the 'have-nots'. The limbic brain might yearn and hope for peace, justice, safety and happiness, but it cannot make it happen because it doesn't know how to create something it hasn't already experienced. Only our PFC can imagine the unimaginable and create what seems completely impossible, both individually and as groups.

§♦

Over twenty years of practice, what I have always found amazing and puzzling is that everyone's executive functions seem to be the same. It appears that qualities such as compassion, empathy, self-awareness, inclusiveness, presence and concern for others, to name a few, don't need to be taught. They are already there, fully formed. All we need is access to these qualities. What comes across as wisdom in the prefrontal cortex, has an ageless and timeless quality.

Our executive functions or abilities seem unrelated to people's history, age or how much life experience they have. I believe and I have observed it in my practice, that the PFC of a sixteen or twenty-year-old is as mature and as wise as that of a much older person. Young people should be listened to and taken seriously for this very reason. There might be a difference in life experience, but the capacity for wisdom seems to be the same. All the executive abilities I described above are already there.

Mistreatment in childhood, drug and alcohol abuse, degenerative brain illness and physical trauma to the front of the brain can damage the prefrontal cortex and our ability to access executive functions. However, the majority of people, even those who had a difficult upbringing still have a functional prefrontal cortex with full access to all the executive functions. My 'guesstimate' is that 80%[12] of human beings have a functional and accessible PFC.

Another thing that I find incredible is that in Eastern religions there has always been an awareness of something special about the area above eyebrow, centre of the forehead. In some traditions it's called the 'third eye', or the 'observer' and in some cultures and religions it is

---

[12] The 20% who do not, includes people with personality disorders. People whose PFC isn't functional will tend to have psychological problems, which will be especially noticeable in relationships. Unfortunately, at present there is no therapy or medical intervention that can correct this.

marked with a jewel or a coloured dot to keep people's attention focused on it. That region, between the eyebrows, has always been associated with insight and enlightenment. I don't know how people could have known this so long ago, but they were right. The limbic brain is very old and the prefrontal cortex is very young by comparison.

The development of our executive functions, including consciousness, do not seem to fit with the evolutionary timetable. They are still a mystery[13].

---

[13] If you are interested in reading more about the origins of the human brain and how it came to be the way it is, look at the work of Professor Bruce Lahn, an expert in human genetics at the University of Chicago. In 2004 he published a paper discussing the accelerated development of the modern human brain. The development of our large and complex brain doesn't quite fit with the standard evolutionary timetable and it is a result of selective activation of a particular group of genes. Scientists are speculating about the possible reasons for this, but they don't yet know how to explain this.

So, What's Our Problem?

If most of us have such great abilities we should be enlightened, self-aware, peaceful and kind to others, inclusive, clear-thinking, rational, peaceful and non-judgemental. We should certainly be better at functioning within relationships. If 80% of us have working PFC capabilities, why are people so unhappy? Why is the world in such a mess? Why do psychotherapists have a job and why are *relationships* so tricky?

Not only do we have two brains that don't 'talk' to each other so well, our problem is that under threat the limbic brain *takes over* and *shuts down* our executive functions. Our evolution has given physical survival priority over everything else, including our need for purpose and meaning and our capacity for empathy and concern for others.

We evolved on a dangerous planet filled with predators and other dangers. When our ancestors were faced with a hungry or angry bear it didn't pay off, in the moment, to empathise with the bear, feel compassion for it or think deep philosophical thoughts. Those who did feel empathy or engaged in deep philosophical thoughts when they faced a predator didn't survive as well as those whose limbic brain 'kicked in', took over and activated the fight-flight-freeze reactions. If the two brains were better connected this would not happen, or at least wouldn't happen so easily. So, on a dangerous planet it didn't pay off to have better connections.

People who have a well-functioning PFC tend to have good access to their executive functions when they are not under threat. But as soon as they experience threat and are triggered, their executive functions recede. The primitive survival system takes over and from that moment on, for the duration of the threat, they are just frightened or angry mammals focused only on their immediate survival. Modern humans have only existed for about 70,000 years. There has not been enough time or enough safety for the two brains to integrate naturally through evolution.

The good news is that it is possible to improve on nature and achieve better integration between the two brains. We have the potential for integration but we need particular relationships to achieve this. The key to integration is in the way that our emotions are handled. Integration between our prefrontal and limbic functions is called 'vertical integration'. If this is achieved in childhood it enables children to grow up with better integrated limbic and executive functions. Better vertical integration can be achieved later in life through training our PFC to handle our emotions in a very particular way. When emotions are handled correctly, it creates physical connections between the two brains.

If parents don't know how to interact with their children's emotions correctly, they grow up as ordinary humans with insufficient vertical integration. Even children who are raised without trauma or serious psychological injuries, will develop into adults whose access to their PFC is compromised each time they are triggered by threat. It's just nature.

Levels of Integration & Relationships

As I explained above, none of us have particularly good integration between our limbic and prefrontal functions. Yet good integration is responsible for what we call maturity. The more integrated we are, the more alive and mature we are and the safer we are to be around. When our vertical integration is better, we can still be fully present and not lose our executive functions, even in the midst of being triggered. It is therefore more likely that we will be able to create supportive, safe, loving and growing relationships with others.

Murray Bowen, the late psychotherapist and contributor to family therapy theory, developed the theory of 'self-differentiation'. He created a scale of differentiation[14] and defined differentiation as 'the amount of self' you have in you. I think of levels of differentiation as representing levels of neural integration between the limbic brain and the PFC. Murray Bowen understood that the higher our differentiation is, the better our relationships will be. But he also said that people attract and are attracted to people with a similar level of differentiation. That makes sense if you remember that we are attracted to what is familiar to us.

People who are near the bottom of Murray Bowen's scale of differentiation — people who are poorly integrated — are not likely to be attracted to people who are much higher on the scale — much better integrated — and vice versa.

---

[14] You can find my adaptation of Bowen's scale of differentiation on my practice website at: http://www.fullyhuman.co.uk/resources/ It is the fourth item from the top.

By looking at the kind of people we are attracted to as partners or friends or the kind of human environment we are drawn to, we can get some idea about our own level of differentiation or integration. It can be humbling. People sometimes think they are more developed than they are, but the truth of how well or poorly developed they are will be in the way they are in relationships with others.

Practice for Improving Vertical Integration

1. Access your PFC by breathing 'into' your eyebrow centre, or just by breathing more deeply. You can close your eyes if it helps. If you meditate or practice mindfulness, use the practices you already know. If you successfully accessed your PFC, you will not feel much. You will feel comfortable in your body, you'll feel 'present' and your thinking will be clear.

2. Once you have gained access to your PFC, try to become aware of what you're feeling. Sometimes it helps to become aware of sensations in the body first and then move on to the emotions. Even if you are not sure about what you are feeling and cannot name your feelings, what you need to do next is validate, soothe and reassure them.

   ✳ **Validating** is saying: **"What you are feeling is OK"**
   ✳ **Soothing** is saying: **"I'm here for you, you're not alone"**
   ✳ **Reassuring** is saying: **"Everything is going to be OK"**

3. Each time you do this, integrative fibres will form between your two brains. The PFC is the adult in us that should have been trained by the adults in our childhood. It's made for the job of running everything in our brain, but if it wasn't trained, it has to be trained now. When it validates, soothes and reassures it 'tells' the limbic brain that it's doing its job.

4. If it feels easy to do, then you have successfully accessed your PFC. If it feels difficult then you are still in your limbic brain. Stop, rest, breathe, try again another time. We don't want the limbic brain trying to validate, soothe and reassure itself. This is what most children are forced to do and it does not contribute anything to integration.

5. The purpose of this practice is not to change feelings, suppress or control them. The purpose is relationships. When adults do this with children they make them feel safe and, therefore, loved and create a strong bond with them. This bond is mirrored inside our brain between the PFC and the limbic brain. What we want to achieve is a better 'relationship' between our two brains.

6. Over time, you develop the ability to do this instinctively and automatically every time you feel anything.

7. This practice is much harder to for people who have trauma. Trauma causes the limbic brain to be triggered a lot and the limbic brain can therefore be more dominant. (People with trauma might find it beneficial to work on this with a skilled therapist).

8. Developing better vertical integration paves the way to integrating painful or traumatic memories and experiences. It should be the *first step* in everyone's therapy. The better the vertical integration is, the *safer* and more efficient the process of recovery will be.

9. Vertical integration improves with practice because practice and repetition reinforce neural connections. As vertical integration improves, the recovery from familiar triggers becomes much quicker. Over time familiar triggers weaken and many disappear completely. Good vertical integration is associated with what we think of as maturity and being 'together'.

10. It's helpful to practice with other people. You can practice validating each other and reminding each other to do this. If you have children or young people in your life, practice with them. As you see the changes in them, you will be more likely to believe that this practice works.

Triggers, emotional 'landmines', flashbacks

I think of triggers, psychological 'landmines' and flashbacks as a form of memory. Unlike a straightforward memory that has no 'charge' or 'sting' in it (for example, remembering that last Saturday you mowed the lawn in the morning and then spent some time with friends at the market), triggers, landmines and flashbacks are usually emotionally charged.

They can feel all-consuming to the point where you can lose touch with the here-and-now. In the moment you experience them you no longer remember that the people around you are people you love and who love you. You forget who you are now and you can feel and also behave in ways that hark back to previous times, circumstances and places. Triggers, landmines and flashbacks in some form or another are the main reason that bring people to therapy. Triggers, landmines and flashbacks are also the main cause of relationship problems.

The more traumatic and challenging the past, the longer and more uncomfortable the recovery from it will be. Psychological trauma is the hardest to recover from[15]. But between full-on trauma and a relatively mild upbringing, there is a sea of possibilities.

Triggers, emotional landmines and flashbacks are really the same thing. They can vary in intensity and the levels of emotional distress they can stir up for people. The worse the trigger, the more 'far gone' we are temporarily. No two people are the same, including children who grow up in the same family. What is wired into our limbic brain is based entirely on our unique past experiences.

Most flashbacks are emotional rather than visual. You might have seen in films, especially about soldiers in combat, that flashbacks can appear as a series of visual images. The former soldier spends a leisurely sunny Sunday afternoon with his wife and children walking happily along the beach. Everyone is relaxed and enjoying themselves. The next minute a helicopter flies by and the father begins to panic. He might start shouting things that don't seem to make any sense in that moment and that place. He might cower, seek cover, collapse in distress, start running wildly or push people away who try to comfort or come close to him. This is what you see on the outside. Inside his mind, the veteran,

---

[15] See my booklet on trauma in this series.

hears, smells and feels an unintegrated reality from another time that was triggered by the sound of the helicopter.

This is an obvious example. What is less obvious or clear is when a veteran, suffering from post-traumatic stress, is hostile and violent towards his wife and children without an obvious cause in the here-and-now. There might be raised voices in that household, intolerance, harshness, criticism, impatience, little things are too important and small children treated as if they are a big bad enemy. There is no obvious trigger, at least not one that others can see or hear, but it is there.

Triggers, emotional landmines and flashbacks are a big component in relation to addictions. No one wants to re-live bad experiences and repeatedly feel the feelings generated. If someone has too many of those because they come from a difficult background, they might try to medicate themselves through the use of a range of substances.

A lot of people can understand the experience of an ex-soldier. But people don't tend to understand flashbacks or triggers in people whose childhood or life experiences in general do not appear to have been particularly dramatic or awful. But we all have them. This is because almost everyone has experienced something that left an emotional impact on them throughout their childhood and upbringing or later in life, which was not well integrated.

It isn't what happens to us that leaves a lifelong mark, it's how it is handled. Unprocessed experiences remain unintegrated, that is 'raw' and unprocessed in our right brain. We call this 'unfinished business'. We need others, especially when we are young, to help us process things that happen to us. We don't need many, one mature adult who is skilled with emotions is usually enough. For children, ideally, it should be someone significant. We need to be able to talk about what's happened and be heard and validated. When this is available, experiences move across from the right brain to the left brain and become integrated. We develop words and concepts in our left brain to describe what we experienced. Right-left brain integration (horizontal integration) is what happens when we 'make sense of things'.

As experiences become better integrated, the 'sting' goes out of them and they are no longer a problem. If children don't have anyone to talk to, or people handle their experiences clumsily, they remain as a 'raw' unintegrated bunch of feelings, sensations, sounds and maybe images too. These will remain like landmines in the right hemisphere of the brain and they are liable to 'explode' every time something triggers them. People with a less traumatic past might have less of those, or milder ones, compared to people with a difficult past, but they will be there nonetheless.

Most of the problems people have in relationships are caused by the fact that, usually unintentionally, one or both parties trigger something that's sitting unintegrated in their right brain. When their respective triggers are awakened, or in other words, when a particular piece of old circuitry in the limbic brain begins to fire, it is as if both people are transported somewhere else in time or place. They are no longer present in the here-and-now. They no longer see each other. The other might behave as an earlier 'version' of themselves, maybe a threatening or otherwise distressing figure. Neither might be doing anything objectively wrong. But there is some quality to the interaction or environmental context which triggered something difficult from the past. The reaction doesn't have to be explosive. If the original reaction to what was happening was fear or was withdrawal, for example, then when a trigger initiates the person might experience fear and withdraw.

Unintegrated experiences feel very real. When the circuitry fires, we feel everything we felt when the original experience took place. Depending on how integrated or unintegrated significant past events are, they would be triggered more or less often.

In relationships, people make two common mistakes. When they are triggered in the present they either assume that it is all the other person's fault and that the other person is the cause of how they feel. Or, they assume that it is their own fault and that they are in the wrong or are 'bad'. These two common ways of approaching relationship problems not only do not solve anything, they are likely to lead to distance, mistrust, conflict and insecurity in the relationship.

People who assume that it's all the other person's fault, risk blaming, dismissing, controlling and causing hurt that might be difficult to recover from. People who assume it's their own fault, risk dismissing their own inner experience and invalidating themselves. They might suppress their own feelings, opinions or needs. In the longer term this is likely to lead to resentment and distance in the relationship.

Whether you tend to blame yourself or the other person when there is conflict or tension, it's important to pay attention to the intensity of your trigger. An important rule of thumb to remember is that if feelings are *overwhelming*, they are likely to be 90% in the past and only 10% in the present. In other words, feelings that seem out of proportion to the present situation are likely to be a result of a flashback or an old landmine. Feelings that are just about the present and have no links to anything in the past, will not feel overwhelming or particularly intense. They will also fade away fairly quickly and will not be much of a problem.

A Rule of Thumb
If feelings are overwhelming, they are probably
90% in the past and only 10% in the present.

Only when people have clarity about their trigger and regain their perspective, that is once the PFC is engaged again, they will be able to discuss the issue calmly and rationally with the other person. People don't often consider the possibility that the relationships they are in and the old stuff they trigger can help them heal the past.

Triggers can be an opportunity to gain better self-awareness and integrate something from our past. The closer and more important the relationship, the more likely it is to trigger 'unfinished business'. When people bring relationships to therapy, it is because they have not been able to deal with these triggers on their own and they need outside help.

Most people's limbic brain works perfectly. It is important to remember that if it's there, it was 'historically' wired in by our environment. Triggers don't come from nowhere. They are not there because people are trying to be difficult or hurt one another. Whatever it is in the limbic brain that gets triggered, whatever pattern of feeling or behaviour we tend to repeat in certain situations, whatever we think or feel at those times, are all wired in there from our experience. Whether we remember the original experience or not, whether we know someone else's history or not, if it's in there, it used to be out there… The trigger itself and all the feelings it brings up, *are* the memory even if there is no conscious memory of the original event or circumstances.

Things get 'hard wired' into our brain when they are reinforced by repetition. Things can also get hard wired if the event only happened once but if it was especially difficult and involved a great deal of fear or distress. Either way, the limbic brain is doing its job. It maintains a memory in its neural circuitry (on the right side of the brain) so that we can avoid that threat or danger if we come across it again.

The worst thing you can say to someone when he or she is triggered is, "You are overreacting". Of course, they are overreacting, but since their prefrontal executive functions are temporarily disengaged, they are not aware of themselves. What they experience seems real to them in that moment and to be told they are delusional is confusing and undermining. It can play even more into the trigger if it has something to do with being dismissed in the past.

Our limbic brain isn't a 'saboteur' or some 'naughty' part of us that needs to be beaten into shape. It is an ancient system that has evolved to keep us safe and it's doing its job perfectly in most people. The problem isn't the trigger itself or the feelings it brings up. The problem is what caused it to be wired in there in the first place.

Reporting vs Acting Out

Everyone can be triggered and triggers affect how we interact with others in the present. When things are still out of awareness, when the circuitry that fires is still isolated like a well-camouflaged landmine in the middle of a field, it's easy to act out and feel the way we did when the original events were happening.

With enough attention to our inner world, we can acknowledge to ourselves how we feel, validate our feelings 100% with compassion and care and soothe and reassure ourselves that, while things might feel a certain way now, we are in fact safe and are going to be OK.

If we can do this, the very trigger that can be so frightening and so disruptive to the relationship, becomes another opportunity for integration. The relationship would not be harmed and when the trigger begins to run its course, we would be able to *report* what is happening to us to the person we are with. Reporting is very different from acting out. It is harmless. All you are doing is telling someone else about your trigger but you do not act on it.

It's the difference between screaming. "I'm fed up with how you are always too busy to listen to me. You just don't care. If you loved me you would…" And saying, "You know, right now I can feel myself triggered into my old fear that people don't care about me. It's what it was like when I was growing up. Everyone was always in their own world and no one paid any attention to me. It makes me feel lonely and frightened".

If people are able to *report* what's going on with them instead of act out, if they can ask for what they really need in that moment, then old circuitry in their limbic brain would not cause harm in their present relationship. Prefrontal awareness and the ability to report can even enhance relationships. We can learn more about each other when we report instead of act out and we don't harm the relationship. When we report instead of acting out, it is easier for others to offer their support and understanding.

If people are able to reach the level of integration that enables them to report instead of act out, they would also realise that what the old circuitry is asking for is not something that can be given by others. Other people can be there, alongside us while we ourselves offer ourselves what we need. As we validate, soothe and reassure our own inner world that circuitry will continue to integrate and in time the trigger will weaken and can disappear completely.

If the other person happens to be a child or anyone else with whom we are *not* in an equal relationship, it's especially important to ensure that we report (if appropriate) and not act out. Children, or anyone else who is less powerful than we are, must never feel that they have to take care of our old childhood needs or pain.

Parents who act out their triggers on their children and demand (openly or unconsciously) that their children make it better for them in some way, are causing harm. This is how things are passed on from a parents' past to their children's developing brains.

'Crimes' against relationships

There are two things I consider 'crimes against relationship', any relationship. One is disloyalty, some form of betrayal of the other. The second is alcohol and other substance abuse. In therapy we have a much better chance of helping people sort out relationship problems if people do not commit either of these 'crimes' against their relationship. People can have problems with each other, but as long as certain lines are not crossed, there is a lot that can be done.

Betrayal

Betrayal comes in many forms but it almost always involves a violation of the boundaries of a relationship. In monogamous intimate relationships, the most common form of betrayal that I come across in my practice is infidelity, emotional and/or physical. Infidelity can involve a sexual relationship with someone else. But it can also mean developing a close emotional relationship with someone else while in a committed monogamous relationship. This means that one partner might be developing a stronger attachment with a person outside the relationship than the attachment they have with their partner.

This is only one example of betrayal. Other examples of betrayal are violation of confidentiality, that is sharing information that is privileged with someone outside the relationship without permission. Financial or other forms of scamming by someone who 'presents' as a good friend or supportive colleague, or just someone you believed you could trust.

In family relationships, a common form of betrayal is when members of the family side with an abuser instead of the victim. Many victims of abuse within the family are betrayed twice. The first betrayal is by the abuser, often a close family member, parent, grandparent, uncle or aunt, a sibling or another relative who they should expect to trust. The second betrayal is committed when family members side with the abuser instead of the victim.

If you go to the core if it, betrayal is about damaging the attachment that should exist between people in relationship. We trust when we believe we are securely attached. Trust means believing that we know what we can expect from the other person, that they are on our side and 'have our back'. Betrayal involves a complete violation of that trust.

Our prefrontal cortex can cope with betrayal. It will be disappointed but it will be OK. The limbic brain is another story. Betrayal can wreak havoc in the limbic brain. It often feels like a complete disaster because it shatters our image of reality, which is linked directly with our survival. When people are betrayed they can feel like they are going to die, that they will not survive it.

It is common for people to feel like it is somehow their fault that they trusted in the first place, or that they somehow brought it upon themselves. But we all need trust and attachment and betrayal is *never* the fault of the victim, only of the person committing the betrayal. Betrayal of trust of any kind will leave the limbic brain of the injured party suspicious and deeply wounded. In many cases it is traumatising and it would be very hard for the injured party to trust new relationships. The reason I call betrayal a 'crime against relationship' is because it can cause damage that often cannot be repaired and that can reverberate sometimes for generations. The emotional injury from betrayal can often lead to complicated grief.[16]

It's really hard to come back from betrayal, any betrayal. Once the trust is broken and the attachment is compromised, it's anyone's guess whether there will be a way back. Some relationships make it and some don't.

Alcohol & Drugs

I don't have a moral position on alcohol or drugs. I am not religious and do not believe it is morally 'evil' or 'wrong' to consume alcohol or drugs. But consumption of any amount of alcohol shuts down our executive functions, which are crucial for our relationships. Many drugs have the same effect.

People often tell me that having a drink 'relaxes' them. Because alcohol shuts down the prefrontal cortex and the executive functions it gives us, I think the only thing that is really happening is that they lose their *awareness* of how they feel, so temporarily they feel more 'relaxed.' They just feel, but they don't *know* they are feeling. Just observe people who drink. They clearly feel everything. People can see that they are happy, sad, angry, seductive. In fact, their feelings are out of control

---

[16] I have a section on complicated grief in my booklet on grief and adjustment to change.

because they lose the ability to regulate them. They, however, think they are relaxed because temporarily they lose their awareness and don't know they are feeling. You don't have to be completely intoxicated to lose executive functions. This starts as soon as we put any amount of alcohol into our system.

Because alcohol (and drugs) alter, damage or compromise the human brain, they do direct harm to relationships. As you already know, the brain we take with us into a relationship has a direct and far-reaching impact on other people.

Long term consumption of alcohol can compromise neuroplasticity, the ability to change the architecture of our brain. This is tragic because it means that people can lose their very ability to change. Even if people see they need to change and even if they really want to change, they might not be able to do it because their brain won't let them anymore. In safe and healthy relationships, it is crucial to be able to hear and take in feedback from others about ourselves. We all have to be prepared to make the effort to change things in ourselves that might be harmful to others. Even with the best of intentions, people who have been long-term drinkers often can't do it. This means that the relationship itself cannot change. If you are with someone who cannot change, this means that things can never get better or be any different than they are now.

People who are addicted to alcohol or other drugs make their relationship with their preferred substance more important than their relationship with others. Consciously or not — usually not — they are unavailable to be in full relationships with others.

No child or young person should ever be exposed to people who drink or take drugs. It is terrifying for a child to look into the eyes of an adult whose prefrontal cortex is shut down. If the PFC is shut down it is like the person isn't there anymore and there is nothing more frightening for anyone than looking into the eyes of a 'zombie' let alone a child or young person. I have zero tolerance for parents or any adults who drink in the presence of children and delude themselves that they can still interact with them or that they are doing no harm.

I don't think there is any need for me to discuss the harm from violence, verbal or physical, poor judgement or other out-of-control behaviours fuelled by alcohol or drugs. If people want to harm themselves with alcohol or drugs that's their business. But when they are in relationship with others, especially children and young people, they have a responsibility beyond themselves[17]. If people cannot relax or have fun without the use of substances, I think they need to do something about it. It suggests that something isn't right in their world externally, internally or both.

---

[17] I have never had a drug or alcohol problem but back in 1999 I stopped consuming alcohol completely. It just felt like it was not good for me and my body didn't want it. Over the years I have become increasingly aware how important being teetotal is for the long-term integrity and development of my brain.

Co-dependency

The idea of co-dependency has been around for a long time and I am sure some readers will be familiar with it. Co-dependency is traditionally associated with relationships where one or two of the people have an addiction. But not all co-dependencies involve an obvious addiction. One way of understanding and describing co-dependency is to think of it as relationship where there is an unspoken and often unconscious contract: *"You take care of my inner child and I'll take care of yours"*.

Co-dependency is a relationship between two people who *need* each other. They are not adult, but are operating from a younger version of themselves in their limbic brain. Like children, they do not feel like they are choosing this but rather they don't have a choice about it. "I can't live without him/her" is a common sentiment in co-dependency.

It isn't wrong to need others. We're relational creatures so we all need other people. But in co-dependency there is a kind of desperation about the need for the other. It's the same as the need a child feels towards those who are entrusted with their care. Children are vulnerable and cannot survive without adults. It's natural for them to feel a desperation about their attachment because they really do not have a choice if they want to live.

When we operate out of our limbic brain we don't feel like it would be nice to have relationships with other people. Rather it would feel as if our very life depends on it, like we *must* have other people *in order to survive*. Not to be in relationship would feel desperately lonely, life-threatening and therefore terrifying.

When adults are not well integrated they operate most of the time 'out of' their limbic brain. A very young version of them is in charge of their life and it can be terrifying. People in co-dependencies can look like adults but they are not and they often do not feel they can manage an adult life with all its associated pressures and responsibilities.

Relationships based on co-dependency are filled with anxiety. The anxiety or fear that exists in co-dependencies is the same kind of fear that exists in the psychological world of children. All children worry about themselves and their survival. [18] Anxiety in co-dependent relationships is often managed with plenty of escapist activities. Co-dependencies can be distant or enmeshed, but either way they are likely to be exhausting.

They also tend to be rigid. There is no flexibility or space to grow or develop. If one partner in a relationship begins to grow, it can increase the other person's anxiety, which can lead to pressure on the other to not change.

People who have had a co-dependent relationship with someone for a long time do not tend to do so well when the other person dies or becomes unavailable to them for other reasons. They can become bereft and feel lost, frightened and depressed. It's similar to how a child would feel if their caregivers just disappeared and left them entirely on their own.

The terror people feel in this situation can be hard to describe. To the outside world it would look like a complete breakdown and mental health crisis. I believe that a good percentage of old-age depression and mental health crises and breakdowns have something to do with losing a co-dependent relationship.

Co-dependencies can be described as **A-Frame** or **Lean-To** structures. [19] A-Frame is when people 'lean' on each other equally. They cannot stand upright on their own. They feel like they are totally dependent upon one another for survival and cannot live without the other. If one of them 'straightens' a bit and becomes less dependent, there is a risk the whole structure will collapse. Without the mutual 'leaning' there can be no relationship.

---

[18] That's why it is so important to make sure we help children feel as safe as possible rather than make their natural fears worse. People tend to romanticise childhood and often associate it with happiness and a carefree approach to life. But the truth is that all children live in fear. We experience fear from the moment we are born. Research in epigenetics suggests that when mothers experience fear and insecurity during pregnancy we might experience fear even before we are born. This is why it is so important for adults to provide children consistently with secure attachment and safety. To grow up in circumstance where fear is reinforced due to abuse, neglect or an inability to bond emotionally and securely with anyone is unbearable for a child and it is the main cause of trauma.

[19] The A-Frame and Lean-To models are inspired by an idea from *Really Relating* by David Jansen & Margaret Newman.

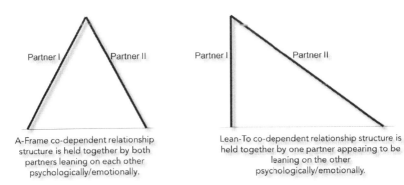

A-Frame & Lean-To Co-dependency Relationship Structure

Partner I · Partner II

Partner I · Partner II

A-Frame co-dependent relationship structure is held together by both partners leaning on each other psychologically/emotionally.

Lean-To co-dependent relationship structure is held together by one partner appearing to be leaning on the other psychologically/emotionally.

In the Lean-To model it can appear as if one partner is leaning on the other. It can appear to be a relationship between a person who is 'strong' and 'together' and a person who is 'unwell' or 'weak'. I am saying 'appear' because in reality there is a co-dependency and although one appears strong, *both* partners are in fact dependent on one another.

If the person who appears weak and dependent 'straightens' out, becomes stronger and less dependent, the one who appeared 'stronger' and more 'together' would collapse, which can cause the relationship structure to collapse. The 'stronger' partner only appears stronger and together because they are held upright by the dependency of the other. In other words, in a Lean-To co-dependency, the 'strong' side is dependent on the other's dependency.

In these kinds of relationship there is often an unconscious agreement between the two people. One might keep themselves dependent and unwell for the benefit of the other's role as competent and strong.

This can be seen in relationships where there is alcoholism or drug dependency. The non-addicted partner might say that they want the other one to clean or sober up. But when the addicted partner tries to recover from their addiction, the partner would unconsciously sabotage it in subtle but effective ways. This is why the non-addicted partner is often called an 'enabler'.

A relationship like this can exist between siblings where one is considered stupid and incompetent and the other smart and successful. If the 'stupid' one is revealed not to be so stupid after all, by for example, going to university and doing well, the other would become anxious because their role as the smart and competent sibling is now threatened.

In co-dependencies there is a lot of 'us' and not enough 'I'. These are relationships where individuality and difference are not tolerated well. When differences become apparent they cause a great deal of anxiety and are, therefore, suppressed quickly.

There can be a lot of conflict and volatility as each partner constantly watches the other for any sign of 'abandonment' of the structure. But there can also be a great deal of suppression and avoidance of conflict. "We never fight", "we always agree on everything" are statements I have heard in my therapy room from many co-dependent couples.

People in co-dependent relationships often don't realise they are co-dependent. They might feel something is wrong or they are unhappy or unwell, or are tired of conflict or distance. The co-dependent structure can easily become apparent when people engage in relationship therapy.

A-Frame or Lean-To Collapse

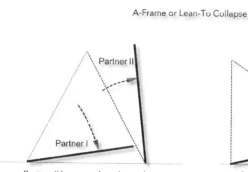

Partner II becomes less dependent causing the A-Frame co-dependent relationship structure to collapse

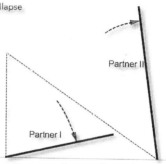

One partner becomes less dependent causing the Lean-To co-dependent relationship structure to collapse

Relationships and Personality Disorders

I am working on a separate booklet on the topic of personality disorders. This section is just a summary of the most important points that I believe people need to consider concerning relationships with people with personality disorders.

In healthy relationships you don't lose yourself. You are supposed to become more of who you are. Bad relationships chip away at who you are, your confidence, your development and your sense of self, among other things. Therefore, by definition, relationships with people who have a personality disorder (PD)[20] are bad relationships.

This isn't a judgement based on prejudice. It is an observation based on science. People who have a personality disorder *permanently* lack the two most important factors that we need for safe and growing adult relationships. They lack *executive functions* and they lack the *neuroplasticity* in the areas of the brain that are relevant to personal growth and to relationships[21]. This is based on emerging data from brain scans and is available from PTA, significant clinical evidence and, in my case, twenty years of clinical experience with relationship therapy and with people who have 'survived' relationships with people with personality disorders.

There is a myth out there that all people with PDs were abused as children, but this is just not true. People can be born with impaired brains as a result of genetics that prevents their PFC and other key areas

---

[20] There are eleven personality disorders known, but the three that are most visible are Borderline PD, Narcissistic PD and Antisocial PD. People with Borderline Personality Disorder (BPD) fear abandonment and seek fusion with others. People with Narcissistic Personality Disorder (NPD) seek adoration more than anything. Those with Antisocial Personality Disorder (psychopathy or sociopathy in everyday language) need to have complete control over others. People with PDs experience deep panic when they don't get what they want and they tend to act out. The type and amount of damage they do to others depends on how much positional power they have, on the type of the disorder and the particular circumstances. All people with PDs lack empathy and other executive functions and are therefore dangerous. No one knows exactly how many people with PDs are out there. My guestimate is that about 20% of the general population has one of the three PDs above.

[21] These two factors (a working PFC and neuroplasticity) are at the heart of how you can assess whether a person really has a PD, or if they are 'just' traumatised. People who have trauma can sometimes have traits similar to people with PDs. But if you assess people properly you will find evidence of executive functions and neuroplasticity in the key areas relevant to development and growth in people who are very traumatised. You will not find it in people who genuinely have a PD.

of the brain from developing properly. Some people might have the genetic pre-disposition for this, which can get expressed through what happens to them. It doesn't have to be abuse. It can be just having to share family life and parents' love and attention with siblings, which children with PDs find intolerable. People can also suffer permanent damage to the PFC and to their neuroplasticity through drug and alcohol abuse, or as a result of an accident or illness.

Not everyone who has been abused will develop a PD although they are likely to develop post-traumatic stress. If the executive functions are there (the PFC developed as it should) and they have good neuroplasticity in key areas, people with trauma can recover. People with PDs permanently lack those. Skilled mental health practitioners can, or should be able to tell the difference.

There are plenty of people with PDs out there who have never been diagnosed and enough people who have been diagnosed as having a PD who do not have it. The key is in whether or not executive functions are there and whether the person shows signs of real growth and change over time in response to their relationship with others.

People with PDs are not bad people who deliberately try to hurt others. But unfortunately, they cannot help but do harm. It is what a brain that lacks executive functions does. When the brain lacks 'adult' executive functions, people are at the mercy of their limbic feelings, triggers and impulses.

As I explained earlier, when we are triggered our limbic brain takes over or tries to take over. Once people without a PD recover, their executive functions will be back and they will be able to *see* what they did or said (self-awareness). They will feel appropriate guilt and remorse, understand the impact they had on others and *care* about it, take responsibility for their actions or words and take appropriate steps to make amends.

People with personality disorders cannot do this. It's not because they don't want to, but because they lack the neurological 'equipment'. Imagine trying to force a blind person to see, when the equipment they need for sight is broken. In the case of people with PD, once a trigger is over, they just move on as if nothing's happened, while other people might still be reeling from the shock and hurt of what had just happened and what they were subjected to.

People with PDs always blame others when things go wrong because the executive function that gives us the capacity to take responsibility isn't working. They would lie and re-write 'history' and facts which can make other people feel like they are going crazy. 'Gaslighting' is something that people with a PD do regularly. This causes not just hurt and a sense of betrayal but also a great deal of confusion. It can leave others feeling like they are losing their sense of what is real and what isn't.

As a result of the impairment to the executive functions, people with PDs appear to have the psychology of two to five-year-old children. They are prone to fears and anxieties, even paranoia, a chaotic or rigid inner world and often both. They are deeply dependent and act out without restraint when they feel threatened. They would tend to manipulate situations to redirect attention back to themselves if they feel that they are not sufficiently the centre of attention[22].

People with PDs find it difficult if not impossible to cooperate with others. Among other things, cooperation requires the ability to relate to others properly, appreciate other people's perspective and the ability to see a larger purpose beyond ourselves or our individual needs or desires (all of which are executive functions). Studies and experience show that when a person with a PD is involved in a group process, the process always breaks down.

Like very young children, people with PD are the centre of their own universe. They lack the executive functions of objectivity and the capacity to see others as separate beings. In fact, the experience of others as separate can be deeply frightening to people with PD and they will fight any sign of it, just like a three-year-old can get 'narky' with mother when she pays attention to a friend or a sibling. Like small children, people with PDs perceive others as objects, *resources* that are there to help them survive, not as people in their own right. Unless you 'work' for them, you are either no use to them, or you are an enemy.

People with PDs can be loving, but in the way that small children are loving. If you are there for them and give them what they want, they 'love' you. But the moment they think you are not, they can 'turn'.

---

[22] A great film about Narcissistic Personality Disorder is the 2004 French film, *Look At Me* (French: *Comme une image*). I recommend it if you want to see a good film and learn something about what it's like to have a parent who has Narcissistic Personality Disorder. It's defined as a drama-comedy but there is nothing funny about it in my opinion.

'Love' can turn in an instant into hatred, rage, abuse, violence, toxicity, sabotage, sullenness, drama or control among other things.

People with PDs often accuse others of abusing them simply because they don't give them what they want or they challenge them. Because of the lack of the executive function of self-awareness, people with PD react with intense negativity and can be unpleasant and cruel to anyone who tries to get them to 'see' what they are doing or to see the other person's point of view. For a person with a PD to reflect on themselves or their actions is like demanding that a three-year-old think rationally and have self-awareness when these faculties are clearly not available to them. They retaliate because they cannot do this and it makes them feel threatened. From their perspective the other person is just 'mean' to them.

Those in relationship with someone with a PD won't even know what they did 'wrong' to trigger the other person. In all likelihood they did nothing wrong, but something in the dynamic made the PD partner feel threatened. Because of the lack of executive functions, it is not possible to sort anything out with someone who has a PD.

People in relationship with those who have a PD feel responsible for them and tend to be preoccupied with them in the same way that adults are with small children who are in their care. This is a problem in adult relationships where both people need to have autonomy, individuality and space to grow, as well as connectedness. This hints at the kind of relationship that is possible with someone with a PD. The only relationship possible with a person with a PD is one-sided. It is similar to a relationship between a carer and a person in their care, or a parent and child. It is not an equal, adult relationship and never can be. This is one of the reasons that it is so harmful for children when one or both of their parents have a PD. From a very young age they are forced to become their parents' parent.

This is also one of the reasons why people with PDs are so difficult to leave. They either won't 'allow' others to leave them. They'll beg, make promises or threats, threaten suicide, etc. or others would just feel too guilty to 'abandon' them. They generate an impression and express this via emotional manipulation that they cannot manage without you in the same way that a small child does. People who naturally have empathy find it difficult to abandon people who appear to be suffering. They also would like to believe that things can get better because they know they can reflect and change and therefore tend to think everyone else can too. The sad thing is that people with PDs are not able to change. It's not because they don't want to but because their brains lack what it takes. (If people can change in a lasting way this means they do not in fact have a PD.)

Relationship therapy, when one of the partners has a personality disorder, is highly inappropriate because it is likely to increase the harm done to the other person. Mediation is also highly inappropriate in such work as it can harm the non-disordered parties and it is highly unlikely to lead to any useful results. Any process that encourages communication between two people is likely to break down if a person with a PD is involved because they are unable to 'reverse roles' with others and see what it's like to be in the other person's position.

The only strategy that might achieve some kind of outcome involves setting strong boundaries. But just as two to five-year-olds tend to challenge the boundaries they are given and often violate them, so will people with PDs. The more power people with PDs have, the more likely they are to violate boundaries and get away with it. I believe people with Personality Disorders must *never* be given power over others.

We don't yet know how to 'fix' personality disorders and I do hope that someday neuroscience will advance to the point where we will be able to repair the parts of the brain whose impairment is responsible for what we call personality disorders. This is for the sake of those who have PDs and those who are affected by them.

The Mirror Neurons

When I started on my journey to recover from the legacy of my own traumatic childhood and later when I was training to become a therapist, the usual wisdom was that no one can 'make you' feel anything. The idea was that all our feelings are entirely and always our own. These self-development 'gurus', self-help books, facilitators of personal development courses and many good therapists meant well. They tried to emphasise the importance of taking responsibility, instead of blaming others for our problems.

But they were wrong. Other people *do* make us feel things. We do it to each other all the time and it happens from the moment we are born. It's incredible in fact how much other people's inner experience can affect and shape the way we feel and perceive reality and how much it can wire itself into our brains. This happens with the help of a network of neurons in our brain called the 'mirror neurons'. The mirror neurones are a relatively recent discovery in humans and other primates. They not only make us feel other people's feelings and inner states, we experience them *as if they're our own*. We mirror each other, or *resonate* with each other. If someone feels sad, we don't just feel their sadness, we experience it as if it is our own sadness.

Our mirror neurons must have played a significant role in our survival and evolution, which is why they are still with us[23]. If a baby feels hungry, uncomfortable or distressed, the mother's (or other caregiver's) mirror neurons will resonate with the baby's inner experience and she will experience what the baby feels as her own inner experience. If it works well, it will (hopefully) move the mother or caregiver to meet the baby or child's needs. Mothers and babies whose mirror neurons resonated better together and were better attuned to each other probably enabled those babies to survive better into adulthood.

---

[23] The way evolution works, the qualities and abilities we have with us now were either helpful to our survival, or didn't get in the way of it. For example, nipples on men serve no purpose at all but they were not selected out because they were not a problem for the survival of our species. If they were a problem the particular genes that are responsible for them would have been 'selected' out as males without nipples would have survived better and longer to pass on their genetic makeup to the next generation.

You might recognise the following scenario or something similar. One minute you feel happy and relaxed. Then you bump into someone you know, strike up some small talk and before you know it you feel anxious, depressed or irritable. It can be disorienting especially if you felt very differently just before you bumped into that person. If you don't know about your mirror neurons and what they do, your brain might try to explain to itself why it's suddenly feeling so dreadful. It can get complicated, especially if the person you mirrored is someone important to you.

Because most people do not yet know about their mirror neurons, they don't automatically assume that those feelings came from the other person. (If they do suspect that, they probably doubt themselves…) We don't yet have mastery over this and cannot easily differentiate between what comes from others and what belongs with us.

While the mirror neurons play such an important role in our survival, they also make us vulnerable. Children do not have what we call 'boundaries.' They cannot 'block' their mirror neurons and choose to not feel someone else's feelings. They have to survive, so their mirror neurones are always there doing their thing. Whatever feelings and inner states happen to be in a child's environment, they will experience as their own. The more important the relationships are and the more attached the child feels, the more significant the resonance will be. Even with the best of intentions, adults cannot prevent their inner experience from being experienced by their children as their own. It is simply a function of our evolution.

A lot of parents think they are 'sparing' their children by trying to cover up or hide it when they feel sad, anxious, angry or distressed. But the way the mirror neuron system works means that even if parents think that they are pretty good at covering up what they feel, all they manage to do is to confuse their children. Children feel their parents' feelings as their own anyway. But when the parents hide them and do not acknowledge them, children may feel bad and not understand why.

Many parents' permanent inner states resonate with their children *repeatedly*. Repetition reinforces neural connections and leads to the development of neural networks in the brain. Those who have grown up around troubled or complicated people, people with personality disorders, unresolved traumas or other mental health issues, could face a particularly tough challenge as adults. All of us can occasionally have a bad moment or day. If we are reasonably OK, this will not be a regular pattern and we will recover soon enough. Troubled people however, might experience cyclical, regular ups-and-downs, like for example, a traumatised parent who regularly descends into a 'dark place', or a person with a personality disorder who 'blows hot' and 'cold'.

Their children (or anyone else affected by them) will not just experience the occasional upset mirrored 'into' them. This will eventually become reinforced. Repetition wires the brain permanently and so repeated experiences, whether positive or negative, become quite literally a part of the physical makeup of the brain. The brain we leave home with is in fact a physical representation of the world we grew up in and everything that was in it, including 'bits' of our parents or other adults who raised us.

Anything we are not conscious of in ourselves, any blind spots we might have, can become a part of other people's inner life, or at least affect them. No one is asked to be 'perfect' or 100% 'sorted'. That's not possible. But to be safe in relationships and to wire 'good' things into other people's brains, people must have a commitment to their own personal development. It is, or should be, a job requirement for all parents.

Mirror Neurons & Empathy

Resonating with someone else's feelings and inner world is a form of basic empathy. Feeling someone else's inner world gives us a good sense of what it's like to be the other person at that moment. This basic empathy seems to me to be different from our executive capacity for empathy.

Our executive, 'higher' capacity for empathy gives us the ability to also *care* about what someone else is feeling. There are people out there who can resonate with others, but they might not care about how the other person feels, or worse, they might even 'exploit' such knowledge in ways that harm others.

I suspect that, as with any ability we have, some people have more sensitive mirror neurons than others. We are all probably somewhere on a spectrum of mirror neurone sensitivity. People who seem to feel other people's feelings more strongly, probably have a more sensitive mirror neurons system.

Experience shows that when we feel under threat or are grieving, or otherwise not well, we might not resonate so well with others. This means that at those times, even otherwise sensitive people, might come across as less empathic or sensitive to other people's feelings and inner states. But whatever people's abilities are, they will be back when the grief is over and when they feel better.

Mirror Neurons & Abuse

When people are abused or harmed, they do not just suffer the obvious effects of being sexually interfered with, or being neglected, beaten, threatened, frightened, criticised or yelled at regularly. Because of the mirror neuron system, I believe that people are abused not only by what is done to them, but also by their abusers' feelings and inner world, which can become a part of their own. It's not surprising that when abuse victims engage in psychotherapy, they often have to 'reclaim' or even recreate their entire sense of themselves and become separate from the person or people who abused them.

In an abusive environment the victim experiences a major and often recurring threat to their survival. Because the mirror neurons are there to support survival, they resonate with the feelings and inner states *of the abusive person* even more strongly and more quickly than those of others. This is part of how children and adults adjust to the abuse and how they try to manage it in order to survive it.

A similar thing happens when people are not directly abused but witness the abuse of others. The witness' mirror neurons will resonate with all the feelings and inner states of both the abuser and the victim. It seems to me that this is one of the reasons that witnessing abuse can have a very similar effect to being directly abused.

If the abuse is not a one-off experience but is repeated (as is the reality for so many victims) the feelings the victim feels (that belong with the abuser) will be reinforced every time the abusive contact or pattern occurs. Just as I explained above, repetition leads to reinforcement of neural patterns and the creation of hardwired neural networks. This is the main reason that abuse is so hard to recover from.

People who are capable of abusing others, who lack sufficient empathy to stop themselves before they do harm, probably have a complicated inner world. It is likely to contain a toxic 'cocktail' of emotions that can 'absorbed' in a powerful way through the victim's mirror neurons.

Talking about the psychology or feelings of abusers or otherwise harmful people is not an excuse for their behaviour.

An explanation is never an excuse!

Please do not take anything I say to mean that I excuse people's bad behaviour because of what happened to them in the past or how their brain is structured. I hold all able-brained adults responsible for their behaviour and for how they impact on others.

If it is too late to make amends for the impact you might have had on others in the past, then you can at least work to become the kind of person who will not do that again to anyone. To become harmless, we must all continually work to integrate whatever it is in us that could impact negatively on others through our behaviour, or the feelings and inner states we expose others to.

Mirror Neurons & Adult Relationships

As adults our partner becomes our primary attachment figure and our mammal brain assumes that our survival depends upon them. We all 'transmit' and 'receive' emotions and inner states through our mirror neuron system. The closer we are to someone and the stronger the attachment we have to them (secure or not), the more likely we are to mirror them and experience their inner states as our own. In other words, the more we believe there is at stake for us, the more we mirror.

In the section on triggers I explain how one partner's triggers can affect the other partner and how things can sometimes go wrong between people when they are both triggered at the same time. The mirror neuron system is partly what causes this 'ricochet effect': one person triggers the other and vice versa. They then react by fighting or arguing, or walking away and cutting off.

Our emotions are intended to affect others, particularly in times of distress. This is because when we are very young and dependent on others, our lives might depend on this. If a baby is in distress for whatever reason and no one notices, they could die. The more immature people are and the less self-aware, the more likely they are to 'spill out' their inner world onto others. People with poor self-awareness who don't know what they are feeling, or who don't know how to ask for what they need, can end up asking for what they need the wrong way by acting in a way that makes others feel what they feel.

People who don't know how to ask for what they need, instinctively act on the other person's mirror neurons. It's as if they are unconsciously trying to induce their own feelings and inner states in others. The principle is that if they can make their partner feel what they feel, the partner (like a parent with a baby) might meet that need. In adult relationships this will often backfire or damage the relationship. It will lead to confusion and resentment in other people, not to mention a feeling of being used and drained. Trying to meet needs indirectly when people don't have functional ways of asking is the definition of manipulation. Most manipulative behaviour is unconscious, but it is harmful all the same and it employs the mirror neurons. Babies and children use the adults around them and that is OK and to be expected. But if adults do that to other adults, it's not.

Exercise in Mirror Neurons Mastery

Over the years I have developed a way to identify the difference between what is mine and what are other people's feelings and inner experience. When I have an emotional reaction to another person (it doesn't have to be a 'bad' one) I breathe deeply and ask myself one question:

'How much of what I am feeling is mine and how much is his/hers?'

This simple question seems to engage the PFC and leads to clarity. It makes us know what other people are feeling but we do not feel it as our own. (You might think my idea is too simplistic, but it works. I invite you to test it and see for yourself.)

Love

Whether we like it or not, we have to accept that we are mammals who also have executive functions. We are therefore capable of two kinds of love, limbic or mammal love and executive or universal love.

Limbic / Mammal Love

Limbic (mammal) brain love is not bad, inferior or wrong. It is what our limbic brain is capable of and it plays a crucial part in the survival of our species. Limbic love is what we call 'attachment' and it is both needs and fear driven. Attachment is by nature conditional and fickle and it is directly linked with our survival and the needs that we associate with it.

Attachment is what children feel towards those entrusted with their care and protection. Children don't have a choice about attachment. They are completely dependent and have to rely on others to survive. Attachment is the connection or bond that children and adults feel towards one another. It is there to guarantee that children will be protected and have what they need so that they can survive. Attachment makes adults feel protective towards the young of our species so that they protect them from harm. It causes children to try to stay close physically and psychologically to those around them to maximise the chances of receiving what they need in order to survive.

Without the proper bond of attachment, adults would not feel protective enough towards children. This would mean that children would not be cared for properly and could come to harm[24].

In adult romantic relationships our limbic brain sees our partner as our primary object of attachment. Although we are no longer children and our survival no longer depends on the adults around us in the same way it did when we are young, our limbic brain transfers our attachment onto our adult partners. In other words, we feel the same bond with our partner that we felt toward our primary carers earlier in life.

Attachment is fickle. When we feel protected or 'close' to those who protect us, we 'love' them. But when we believe that they don't give us what we want or need, when they are not attentive enough to us when

---

[24] Given the huge rates of child abuse and the fact that most child abuse is perpetrated within families it is clear that the process of attachment does not always work the way it should.

we need them to be, when they want to do something else when we want them to be with us or when they seem to not protect us, we could easily lose that 'loving feeling'.

Think of the last time you heard a toddler say 'I hate you' to mum simply because she refuses to buy the ice cream he wants the moment he wants it. When we don't get what we feel we need or want and when, in our mind, this is linked with our survival, we are capable of feeling hurt, pain, fear, anger, disappointment, abandonment and even hatred. At that moment we genuinely feel threatened and insecure. We truly believe that the very person who is supposed to keep us alive and protect us has abandoned us and we are out in the cold[25].

The strength and intensity of attachment in adulthood depends on the type of relationship we are in. The strongest bond is usually in romantic relationships and partnerships. It plays itself out in the most powerful and intense way when we are 'in love' and are filled with the bonding drug *oxytocin*. The role of oxytocin is to make mothers and fathers feel an immediate bond with their new born baby. It makes parents and others close to the baby feel a powerful and irresistible urge to protect him or her. It has to be instantaneous because human babies die very quickly if they are not looked after[26].

Mothers and fathers who bond properly under the effects of oxytocin see their babies as beautiful and perfect. It doesn't matter what others might think about the baby's appearance. To the oxytocin-fuelled parents the baby will appear irresistible, perfectly lovable and they would feel a powerful loving feeling and an irresistible urge to protect their baby and be physically close to him or her. Good levels of oxytocin in parents mean a better chance of survival for the baby.

---

[25] Yes, not getting ice cream at the very moment he craves it and feeling uncomfortable about it can make a toddler feel genuine mortal threat. It's up to adults to understand this and teach their children *gently and thoughtfully* what is a real threat to their survival and what isn't. Children's brains learn from those around them what's worth worrying about and what isn't.

[26] We often feel the same bond with animals that we 'fall in love' with and it can be especially powerful when the animal is young. Some studies have tried to figure out what triggers this bond with our own young and the young of other species. They wanted to know what it is exactly that triggers the oxytocin to begin to flow through our veins. One of the hypotheses has been that it has something to do with the shape of the heads of young mammals that provides a visual cue to begin the process. Whatever it is, it's important that we do feel a protective urge towards our own and other creatures' young because all young need all the help they can get in order to survive.

When people are in love they are in fact flooded with oxytocin. They tend to feel the same instantaneous bond, although they might not yet know each other so well. Everything can seem just perfect. At this stage it is typical to have a strong physical attraction and have plenty of sexual contact.

When people are in love they feel that they 'belong together', that they were 'destined to be together', that they 'were made for each other', are 'perfect' for each other or that they 'complete each other'. All they want is be with each other physically. When people who are in love are separate geographically it can feel like a physical ache. You just want to be together, feel each other physically and protect each other. There are plenty of love songs about this experience because it can be so overwhelming, powerful and pleasurable (at the same time as it can be anxiety-provoking).

A similar thing happens also when we 'fall in love' with a new friend, pet, job, house, or even an object like a car. Initially, they are just perfect for us and can do no wrong. Oxytocin enables us to not see, or ignore any faults in the object of our attachment. Differences are overlooked and we can be blind to or dismiss things that would otherwise annoy us. The question is, what happens when oxytocin wears off…

Everyone knows that, after the high of the 'drug induced' in-love period, 'reality' sinks in. How long this takes varies between people. If you are lucky, oxytocin will remain in your system for about a year. For some people it's less and for others it can be a bit longer. When the oxytocin wears off it can feel like you are suddenly waking up from a dream. Suddenly your partner, (or friend, pet, job, house or car) does not seem so perfect anymore. Now you begin to see the flaws and imperfections and what during the initial in-love period did not bother you so much, can begin to be a problem now.

Imperfections or 'flaws' in partners just mean that you don't agree on everything, that there are differences between you, that you do not see everything, that you have different rhythms and preferences and that you have different needs at different times. This is normal but it can feel deeply disappointing because you still remember feeling that 'they' were perfect when it all started.

Differences or characteristics that originally you might have noticed but dismissed or glossed over thinking, "it's kind of cute that he does that", or "it's not so important and I can live with that", might suddenly stand out. This is the stage in adult relationships when people can feel irritated, hurt and let down by their partners' (friends, job, house, car) 'imperfections'. It is the point where people realise they do not in fact fit so well and they are more different than they realised when they were under the influence of oxytocin. That's when people might begin to think they might have made a mistake, or that the partner might have deceived them and 'miss-sold' themselves.

The truth is we are all a bit dishonest when we fall in love, but not intentionally. Nature makes us more accommodating, patient, generous and adventurous than we might normally be. We tend to present the version of ourselves that fits best with the other person. We all do it.

If we are not well-developed and live mostly out of our limbic brain, we are at the mercy of nature's attachment. As self-aware mammals, it is usually not a recipe for adult mature relationships. People who are predominantly limbic tend to fight a lot or drift apart. They would tend to be preoccupied with their relationship and wonder what happened and why their partner isn't as accommodating, loving or attentive as they used to be. If they look closely at themselves, they'll notice that they too are not quite the same as they were in the 'in-love' stage of the relationship. Many people leave relationships and try again with someone else. But if they are still predominantly limbic and have not integrated enough, they are likely to find themselves in the same place after the oxytocin wears off. We take the same brain everywhere we go…

Executive or Universal Unconditional Love

"I define love thus: The will to extend one's self
for the purpose of nurturing one's own or another's
spiritual growth." — M. Scott Peck. *The Road Less Travelled.*

M. Scott Peck's definition of love is in fact prefrontal love. Unlike our limbic attachment, our prefrontal cortex gives us the capacity to love unconditionally, universally. This means that we are able to love everyone, see others for who they are as separate persons to us, irrespective of what they can do for us, or whether or not they can help us survive.

PFC love is not just a sweet feeling, it might not be a feeling at all. It is a form of being with others, acting in a way that supports their growth and development. We extend the exact same love to ourselves and it is expressed when we validate and listen to our limbic experience and emotions. "Love thy neighbour as yourself" tells us to love others from our PFC not just our limbic brain.

PFC love is unconditional and does not require anything from others. What people perceive as divine love is the same thing and we have the capacity for this in our prefrontal cortex. Just like the rest of our executive functions, this too is a bit of a mystery. People who have good access to the PFC experience this love as a connectedness to everything, to something universal that is outside of them. The goal in philosophies like Buddhism is to cultivate this way of being.

We cannot and must not shut down our attachment. We have a limbic brain and it has its job to do. But the more we integrate our two brains, the better they work together, the more we ensure that the limbic brain is not in charge. When we are better integrated, we ensure that our executive functions, including our capacity for unconditional love, are in charge more of the time.

It is pretty obvious that, when we are better integrated, we will also be able to love others in our lives unconditionally and inclusively. It doesn't mean putting up with everything or ignoring problems. But the way we would act and communicate would be driven by mature love and concern for other people's integrity and wholeness and not just our own need to survive. We will be gentler and more compassionate with others and will not discriminate so easily between people. We can see that everyone is unique and everyone is valuable and has a contribution to make if they are enabled to do that.

When we love properly from our PFC we will act for everyone's benefit, not just those (our family, group or country) upon whom we feel dependent for our survival. The more we act out of our PFC and the capacity for unconditional love it gives us, the bigger the chances that we will create a safer world where everyone is offered a good opportunity not just to survive but to become everything they can become. But it takes integration to get there. If we are not well integrated we will continue to run the world as we do now, according to limbic principles.

Sometimes It's Just Not Right

I had a friend many years ago who believed that any two people can develop an intimate relationship. This way of thinking is common in societies where marriages are arranged. In arranged marriages, partners do not choose each other but are chosen for each other by others and for reasons that are more social than personal. These relationships might not start with falling in love, an attraction or a 'soulmate' experience, but they can develop as people begin to live together. If people end up happy together, that's a bonus, but if not, that's OK too provided they fulfil their obligation to society by having children and functioning as they are expected to by those around them.

In Western societies we choose our partners and our friends. We don't choose our family and if we are employed by others, we don't have a choice about our work colleagues, bosses or people we supervise. It's common for people to feel a sense of failure if things go pear-shaped in a relationship. But sometimes relationships just don't work out and it's no one's fault in particular. I can love everyone unconditionally but it doesn't mean that I would want to live with everyone or be close friends with everyone.

People can work really hard on their relationship but at the end of the day they might not be happy with each other for reasons other than them 'not trying hard enough'. We might start out with the best of intentions but things can turn out different than what we had hoped for or intended. Perhaps there is a fundamental difference in beliefs and values. We do have different personalities and different ways of experiencing the world and interacting with what's in it. We have different interests, preferences, priorities, likes and dislikes.

An important difference between people, that might not be evident at the start of a relationship is how each individual understands what the relationship is for and what it should look like. It's not that either is wrong. They're just different.

Sometimes when people first meet they 'fall in love'. This can happen between friends or colleagues as well. Falling in love in this sense is feeling instantaneous closeness with someone but without knowing much about them. As people get to know each other better, they might find that there are things about the other person they don't like and that for them are a 'deal breaker'.

It can also be that people change over time. Their priorities and beliefs might change as well as how they perceive relationships. They can adopt new activities or hobbies and their physical health might change, which can impact on what they can do and how they function in relationships. Sometimes, as time goes by, people discover that what they want from their relationships is different from what they thought they wanted at the start.

Sometimes it just doesn't work out and it's no one's fault. If people can go their separate ways respectfully it might be sad but no harm has to be done.

Relationship Therapy & Relationship Therapists

Safety in Relationship Therapy

All therapy must offer a safe relational space for people. Without safety, progress towards recovery will be compromised. Safety in relationship therapy must include balance and equality.

Balance

Safe relationship therapy is balanced. The therapist should not side with either partner or be biased in favour of one over the other. Sometimes clients can feel that the therapist is biased but it might not be the therapist's fault. Maybe the client has wiring from the past that makes them feel as if figures of authority always side with others against them. Irrespective of whether it is a client issue or something the therapist is doing wrong, it is crucial that this is discussed openly and safely with the therapist. Good, skilled therapists are trained to work with this kind of exploration. Therapists who respond defensively to your attempt to make sense of what's going on, are not safe to work with.

Sometimes a session might focus on one partner more than the other because this is *what is needed* in that moment or in that stage in the process. But therapists have to ensure that throughout the therapy process the space is divided reasonably equally.

Balance in therapy mirrors how it should be in the relationship outside of therapy. Sometimes one partner needs more attention or care than the other for a period of time. A simple example is if one is not well and needs to be cared for, or if someone is grieving or adjusting to a big life change that does not necessarily involve the partner. Relationships do not work well if, in the long term, there is no balance.

This isn't just true for committed partnerships but for any personal relationship between two adults. Even the nicest, most patient people will get fed up if every time they meet for coffee, their friend only wants to talk about themselves. One of my female clients told me recently, "I have noticed that every time I meet my sister everything is always about her. If I try to say something about myself or what's going on in my life, she changes the subject back to herself or loses interest."

People will only tolerate a lack of balance up to a point and if the other person happens to be going through something significant. But they would expect that eventually, after things settle down, there will be time for them as well.

Equality

Equality can be a tricky concept. I often notice that people confuse being *equal* with being *identical*. Being equal does not mean being identical. Equality in relationship means something very particular. It means that both people involved are *equally valuable* in all aspects of their being.

They both *matter* equally. Their inner worlds matter, their wants, needs and preferences, their values, their beliefs, their opinions, their experiences, their history, their suffering, their grief, their interests, the roles that they play in their lives...*everything* about both partners is *equally valuable*. That's real equality.

People have different needs and different needs at different times. We just cannot be equal in terms of the needs we each have. But the needs of both people in a relationship *must* be considered by everyone involved as *equally important*. Some needs might be more pressing and require special attention at certain times, such as when someone has health problems or they need to grieve, for example. But this does not mean that overall the needs of the other partner in the relationship are less important.

Not all needs can be met and not all needs can be met all the time. One partner's needs might be more urgent and the other partner's needs might have to wait a little. But they are always equally important. If people enter into relationships wired from their limbic brain to believe that their own needs are less or more important than their partner's, I guarantee you there are going to be problems.

In the therapy process equality means that both partners are expected to be *equally committed* to the process and *equally capable* of engaging with it in a safe and productive way. Everyone is wired differently so people often have different areas of development to concentrate on and different 'homework' they feel they should focus on between sessions. But the expectation is that both people would have equal *commitment* and equal *capacity* to engage with the process. If they do not, therapy will not only be ineffective it can also be harmful to one or other of the partners.

Our executive functions are absolutely essential for safe and healthy relationships and for healthy cooperation with others. The executive functions that most relationship therapists would consider fundamental are the capacity for empathy, the ability to see clearly and care about how you impact on others, emotional regulation and self-awareness. If one of the partners is permanently incapable of empathy, or self-awareness or of grasping and caring about how he or she impacts on others, relationship therapy must not be engaged with.

To be safe and healthy, personal relationships between two adults must also include equality of power. This means that both partners have to feel that they have the same amount of power in the relationship. When there is a task to perform, or something to achieve that requires one person to exercise more power, things need to be negotiated. Negotiations are only appropriate where everyone has the same amount of power. If one side is more powerful negotiations are not real. It's just one side imposing their will on the other while maintaining the appearance of fair negotiations.

An imbalance of power between people is often unavoidable. Certain jobs require some people to have more positional and organisational power than others. All adults automatically have more power than children, teachers and lecturers have more power than students, commanding officers in various law enforcement agencies, commanders in rescue services or military forces also have more power than the people they command.

Without some power imbalance it would be difficult to keep children safe, or run an engineering project. Teachers are automatically more powerful than their students simply because they are entrusted with the task of training them and evaluating their performance. But none of these are *personal* adult relationships.

In political science power is sometimes defined as 'the ability to make someone do something they wouldn't otherwise do.' Power is not inherently bad. But power can be abused and often is when it is in the wrong hands. *All* incidents of abuse in *all* contexts involve an imbalance of power. In abusive situations, systems or incidents the more powerful party abuses their power in a way that allows them to *use* another person or persons as a resource for their own purposes without the other person's genuine free consent. Abuse can be economic, physical, sexual, psychological, all of the above and more.

Depending on our childhood environment, our society and the wiring they 'put into' our brain, we might think we are entitled to more power than others because of our gender, our perception of 'race', level of education, because we belong to a certain religion or belief system, because our family happens to have more or because of our social class. We can also be wired to believe that we have less power. When people enter relationships, they bring these pre-wired and often unconscious beliefs with them into the relationship.

For generations, women in the West were at the bottom of the social pecking order. It was therefore normal for many women to assume that they were automatically less powerful than their male partners. No matter how relationships were handled internally, when society considered women unequal to men, that also affected how people interacted with one other in their personal relationships.

Not having personal power is bad for our mental health and it leaves us feeling vulnerable. If there is no open and acknowledged balance of power, people will try to take and exercise power in any way they can. Passive-aggressive behaviour for example, is often discussed in the context of unexpressed anger. But I tend to think of passive aggression as the last resort of someone who feels and/or is powerless.

Personal power is necessary for our survival. If we are prevented from having personal power we will become angry or depressed. Anger is what we feel when we are in a bad situation that is potentially dangerous to us. Anger activates certain physical functions that give us the energy to exercise power to fight off an aggressor or do something about a bad situation that affects us or others. Not having personal power to change a bad situation can also leave us frightened.

Depression is what happens when we have tried to exercise our power but realised that we are in fact *powerless* to change the bad situation or fight off the person or situation that is hurting us. People who suffer genuine depression do believe and often have good reason to believe, that they are powerless over something or someone.

Put simply, power in a personal adult relationship has to be shared equally or the relationship will be harmful to the less powerful partner. In all other relationships where an imbalance of power is unavoidable or even necessary, there must be safeguards in place to prevent the abuse of power by the party who has more of it.

Relationship Therapists

No matter how experienced and talented they are, individual therapists cannot automatically work with relationships. Some of the skills from individual therapy are transferrable to relationship work, but relationship therapy is its own art. Good quality relationship therapy requires its own set of high level and quite complex skills. Therapists *must* have appropriate training and qualifications to practice relationship therapy.

If the information provided by a therapist isn't clear, you need to ask whether they are specifically trained as relationship therapists and how much experience they have in this area. There are a number of ways to find a therapist privately. It is usually a good idea to ask for a recommendation from someone who has been through relationship therapy and who is happy with how it went.

Therapists are human beings, so they too have blind spots, issues and unresolved, unintegrated 'stuff'. They don't need to be perfect, no one ever is. But they must be people who have a total commitment to their own development, growth, healing and integration. Therapists who are not comfortable with their own feelings and internal experience, are not safe. Therapists who avoid their own pain and their own 'unfinished business', who are not open to listening to feedback from their clients, are not safe.

All therapists should be genuine and honest. You need to feel that your therapist is transparent enough so that you don't sit there worrying about what the therapist might be thinking about you or your relationship. I encourage you to ask, if you are worried about it. Mature and safe therapists will not be surprised or taken aback by your question. They will be able to answer it truthfully and honestly and in a way that contributes to the therapeutic process. It's important for your therapist to not be defensive about anything. Therapists should be prepared to respond maturely and helpfully to any question or challenge you have.

You have a right to enquire how your therapist understands relationship therapy and how it works and how he or she sees their role in the process. You should not be left in the dark about the therapeutic approach your therapist is following.

The therapy environment should be rich and flexible. Your therapist should be able to offer a variety of ways to engage with therapy. Not everyone feels comfortable just sitting and talking for an hour at a time.

Some people need to express themselves in other ways. Skilled and experienced relationship therapists are usually trained in a variety of helpful methods and techniques to enable you and the person you came to therapy with to express yourselves and make the most of every session.

About the author

Avigail Abarbanel has been a psychotherapist in private practice since 1999. She started practicing in Australia and in 2010 moved to the north of Scotland where she re-established her practice near Inverness.

Avigail is trained to work with individuals, families, relationships and groups. She is also a clinical supervisor, trainer and writer. Avigail sees psychotherapy as a joint venture between therapists and clients to help people come closer to fulfilling their human potential. She prefers a no-nonsense science-based approach to human psychology and to psychotherapy. She loves working with relationships and is passionate about sharing knowledge.

Registered Member **16797**
MBACP (Accred)

Please visit http://fullyhuman.co.uk for more information about Avigail and her work.

Printed in Great Britain
by Amazon